MEXICO

WHAT EVERYONE NEEDS TO KNOW®

D1023091

MEXICO
WHAT EVERYONE NEEDS TO KNOW®

Second Edition

RODERIC AI CAMP

OXFORD
UNIVERSITY PRESS

OXFORD
UNIVERSITY PRESS

Oxford University Press is a department of the University of Oxford. It furthers the University's objective of excellence in research, scholarship, and education by publishing worldwide. Oxford is a registered trade mark of Oxford University Press in the UK and certain other countries.

"What Everyone Needs to Know" is a registered trademark of Oxford University Press.

Published in the United States of America by Oxford University Press
198 Madison Avenue, New York, NY 10016, United States of America.

Library of Congress Cataloging-in-Publication Data
Names: Camp, Roderic A.
Title: Mexico : what everyone needs to know / Roderic Ai Camp.
Description: Second edition. | New York, NY : Oxford University Press, 2017. |
Series: What everyone needs to know | Includes index.
Identifiers: LCCN 2016055978 | ISBN 9780190494162 (hardcover: alk. paper) |
ISBN 9780190494179 (pbk.: alk. paper)
Subjects: LCSH: Mexico—Politics and government. | Mexico—Economic
conditions. | Mexico—Economic policy. | National security—Mexico. |
United States—Relations—Mexico. | Mexico—Relations—United States.
Classification: LCC JL1281 .C339 2017 | DDC 972—dc23
LC record available at https://lccn.loc.gov/2016055978

1 3 5 7 9 8 6 4 2

Paperback printed by Sheridan Books, Inc., United States of America
Hardback printed by Bridgeport National Bindery, Inc., United States of America

To the Memory of George Grayson, Who Devoted
His Life to Explaining Mexico

CONTENTS

ACKNOWLEDGMENTS   XIII
POLITICAL MAP OF MEXICO   XIV
INTRODUCTION   XVII

PART I MAJOR ISSUES FACING MEXICO TODAY

1 Security and Violence in Mexico   3

Why does Mexico have so much drug violence today?   3

Has Mexico always had a drug problem?   5

Which areas of Mexico are most affected by drug violence, who
are the primary targets, and does the violence spill across the border?   7

How are Mexico's security problems America's problems?   10

What is the origin of the drug cartels and which organizations
are the major cartels?   12

What role has Mexico played in US Northern Command?   14

What do Mexicans consider to be the most important issues facing
the country?   16

Does Mexico exercise political sovereignty throughout the republic?   17

2 Mexico's Economic Development   20

How poor is Mexico?   20

How is Mexico addressing its poverty?   22

What is the economic relationship between Mexico
and the United States?   24

What is the impact of NAFTA on Mexico?   25

What is the state of Mexico's economy today?   28

What kind of economic model does Mexico follow?   30

What does the Mexican economic model teach us
about development?   32

Why is Mexico City so polluted and can this condition be altered?   34

How has Mexico addressed domestic and cross-border
environmental issues?   35

3   Mexico's Political Development   38

When did Mexico become democratic?   38

How democratic is Mexico?   39

Why did Mexico make the democratic transition so slowly?   42

What can Mexico teach us about civil–military relations?   43

Why has Mexico been so stable since the 1930s?   45

What is the impact of the United States on Mexico's political
development and democratization?   46

4   Relations with the United States   49

What is the impact of geography on Mexico?   49

What has happened with immigration to the United States?   52

Could the International Boundary and Water Commission serve as
an institutional model for other issues with the United States?   55

What can the United States do to help Mexico?   57

How has Mexico influenced the United States economically?   59

5   Mexico's Social Development   61

How inequitable is Mexican development and what are
the social consequences?   61

What is the current status of indigenous Mexicans?   63

What are Mexican attitudes toward global environmental issues?   65

PART II HISTORICAL LEGACIES

6 Mexico's Colonial Heritage   69

*How did the Spanish viceroys shape Mexico's political heritage in
the nineteenth and twentieth centuries?*   69

*What was the relationship between church and state in Mexico
and why was it so different from that in the United States?*   71

*What consequences did the colonial relationship between church
and state have for the nineteenth and twentieth centuries?*   73

*What is the most important heritage of Spain's economic system
in Mexico?*   75

How were social class relations determined by colonial experiences?   76

7 The National Period and the Rise
of Liberal–Conservative Conflicts   78

*What were the long-term consequences of Liberal–Conservative
conflicts in Mexico?*   78

*Who started the Mexican–American War and how did it affect
relations with the United States?*   79

Who was Benito Juárez?   81

What was the War of the Reform?   82

Why was the Constitution of 1857 so important?   83

Who was Porfirio Díaz and what was the Porfiriato?   85

*What were the long-term consequences of the Porfiriato
for the twentieth century?*   86

8 The Mexican Revolution and a New Political
Model for Mexico   89

THE MEXICAN REVOLUTION   89

What were the causes of the Mexican Revolution of 1910?   89

Who was Francisco I. Madero?   91

Who really was Pancho Villa?   92

Who benefited most from the Mexican Revolution?   94

*Could Mexico have achieved changes in its structures through
peaceful means instead of violence?*   95

How did the revolution alter political institutions
and civil–military relations? 97

What was the attitude of the United States toward the revolution? 98

What is the Constitution of 1917? 100

What was the cultural impact of the Mexican Revolution on
painting, music, and literature? 102

THE EVOLUTION OF MODERN POLITICAL STRUCTURES AFTER 1920 104

Why did the assassination of President-elect Álvaro Obregón alter
Mexico's political future? 104

What was the influence of Plutarco Elías Calles
on the formation of a modern Mexican state? 106

What is the National Revolutionary Party? 107

Who was Lázaro Cárdenas and how did he influence Mexico's
political model? 109

Why did Mexico nationalize the petroleum industry in 1939? 110

Did Mexico participate in World War II? 112

When did civilian leadership take control of the Mexican political
system? 113

What is the Alemán generation and what were its consequences
for Mexican politics? 115

What is the Institutional Revolutionary Party? 116

What is the Mexican economic miracle? 118

What is the National Action Party? 119

THE DECLINE OF THE INSTITUTIONAL REVOLUTIONARY
PARTY AND THE MEXICAN MODEL 120

What was the Tlatelolco Student Massacre of 1968 and
what were its long-term political consequences? 120

What was the "Dirty War" in Mexico? 122

What was the impact of the 1964 electoral reforms? 123

What were the leading political characteristics of Mexico's
semiauthoritarian model? 125

What were the consequences of the nationalization of the banks in
1982? 126

Did Mexico's economic woes in the 1980s have significant political
consequences? 128

9 Mexico's Democratic Transition 130

How did Carlos Salinas alter the Mexican political model? 130

Why is the presidential election of 1988 a benchmark for
democracy in Mexico? 132

Who is Cuauhtémoc Cárdenas and what is the Party of the
Democratic Revolution? 133

What is NAFTA and how did Carlos Salinas change Mexico's
economic model? 135

Who are the technocrats? 137

When did an opposition party win its first governorship in Mexico? 139

What was the Zapatista uprising of 1994 and what were its
political consequences? 140

What were the consequences of the Zapatistas for civil–military
relations? 141

Why is the presidential election of 1994 considered a second
benchmark in the democratic transition? 143

What was the role of the Catholic Church in the 1994
presidential race? 144

What were the consequences of the assassination of the
Institutional Revolutionary Party presidential candidate Luis
Donaldo Colosio in 1994? 145

How did President Zedillo contribute to the democratic transition? 147

What is the Mexican bailout? 148

PART III MEXICO'S PRESENT AND FUTURE
10 Mexico's Democratic Consolidation 153

POLITICS OF DEMOCRACY 153

Why was the 2000 presidential race essential to Mexico's
democratization? 153

Who is Vicente Fox? 155

What was the Transparency Law? 156

What Is "Amigos de Fox"? 157

What was the role of the private sector in the democratic
consolidation? 158

What are the most important interest groups?   159

What was the role of the media in the process of democratic
consolidation?   161

What role did intellectuals play in Mexico's democratization?   162

FURTHER CONSOLIDATION   163

What happened in the 2006 presidential race and how did it
strengthen Mexican political institutions?   163

Why did Felipe Calderón win the election?   165

Who is Andrés Manuel López Obrador?   166

Why did the Institutional Revolutionary Party win the 2012
presidential election?   168

What is the National Electoral Institute?   171

What do the Mexican people think about the government's war on
organized crime?   173

What impact does the army's mission against organized crime
have on civil–military relations?   176

How do Mexicans define democracy and how committed are they
to democratic governance?   177

What do Mexicans expect from democracy?   178

What is the Pact for Mexico?   180

11   Cultural, Economic, and Social Developments   183

What are Mexican religious beliefs and religious relationships?   183

How is the drug war influencing cultural and religious behavior?   186

What are Mexican attitudes toward gender roles?   188

How tolerant are Mexicans of minority groups?   190

What is Mexico's impact on cultural trends in the United States?   193

12   What Lies Ahead?   196

CHRONOLOGY OF MEXICAN PRESIDENTS, 1964–2018   203
SELECTED SUGGESTED READINGS IN ENGLISH   205
INDEX   209

ACKNOWLEDGMENTS

When Angela Chnapko, my editor at Oxford University Press, approached me about the new series What Everyone Needs to Know, I was struck by the Press's imagination in attempting to reach a broader audience and hopefully educate North Americans and other readers about multiple aspects of specific countries and their citizens. I owe my deep thanks to her for encouraging me to take on the challenge of writing the original work in the midst of three other book projects. I have always pursued the broadest exploration of all things Mexican, from art to intellectuals, during my professional career, and it was worthwhile and rewarding to reeducate myself in many of these areas. Thus, it has been equally valuable to produce a newly revised edition. I also want to thank my wife, Emmy, for reinforcing Angela's enthusiasm for the original project and for agreeing to my pursuit of a new edition in Claremont and Cooper Bay North in the beautiful spring and summer of 2016.

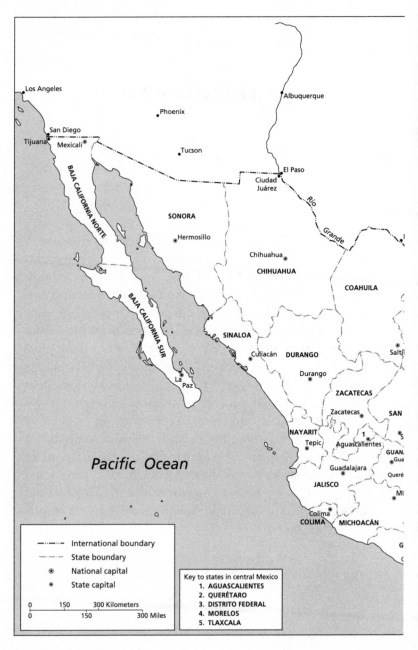

Map 1 Political Map of Mexico

Austin

Houston

Del Rio

San Antonio

HUILA

RIO

Grande

Laredo

Brownsville

Monterrey
**NUEVO
LEÓN**

Saltillo

Gulf of Mexico

Ciudad
Victoria

CAS

TAMAULIPAS

**SAN LUIS
POTOSÍ**

1

lientes

San Luis Potosí

Mérida

YUCATÁN

GUANAJUATO
Guanajuato

2

ra

Querétaro

HIDALGO

Campeche

**QUINTANA
ROO**

Pachuca

Morelia

Mexico City

Toluca

5 Tlaxcala

Jalapa

CAMPECHE

Chetumal

3

MÉXICO

4

Cuernavaca

Puebla

PUEBLA

VERACRUZ

TABASCO
Villahermosa

ACÁN

GUERRERO

Chilpancingo

OAXACA

Oaxaca

CHIAPAS

Tuxtla Gutiérrez

GUATEMALA

INTRODUCTION

Many scholarly friends of my generation who focused on Latin American studies or some other regional specialization have expressed an itch to accomplish two complementary professional, scholarly goals: to write a novel set in their country of expertise and, perhaps even more challenging, to author a textbook. Writing the answers to some one hundred questions about Mexico falls into a similar category. Those of us who are interested in world affairs or the cultures of other countries always have questions we want to ask about them. Thus, it was a welcome invitation to write such a book about Mexico, and I commend Oxford University Press for initiating such a valuable series.

I am into my fifth decade of research on Mexico, having begun my scholarly work in 1966 under the guidance of the late historian Mario Rodríguez, a distinguished Central Americanist. He would have approved of this project, which brings together academic interests from a variety of disciplines. In the first part of the book, I address a series of provocative questions raised implicitly in most recent media accounts, questions that have come up repeatedly in my public speaking engagements among general audiences and students and, surprisingly, in the 2016 Republican presidential primary and during President Donald Trump's first weeks in office. Some of these questions address difficult political and security issues Mexico faces, issues that naturally affect the United States. Because Mexico and the United States share a nearly two-thousand-mile border and a two-century contentious history that ended in Mexico losing half of its national territory to its northern neighbor, our relationship with Mexico, including the various factors, ranging from cultural to economic, that influence both countries, also receives significant attention.

After touching on much of Mexico's historic, political, social, economic, and cultural development during its colonial era and the formative decades of the nineteenth century, the chapters in the second part of the book focus on the impact of Mexico's decisive revolutionary decade of 1910–20, recognized in numerous bicentennial and centennial celebrations in both countries during 2010. To conclude, I answer numerous questions about how Mexico's democratic transition came about, a transition that lagged behind most other countries in the region. In the final part, I explore a number of questions focusing on where Mexico finds itself today as it undergoes changes in the process of democratic consolidation. It is my hope that readers will find their interest sufficiently piqued by the answers to delve further into Mexico's fascinating culture and history and its impact on the United States. Finally, a brief, highly selective bibliography of English-language publications, including works by numerous Mexican authors, introduces readers to resources offering a wide range of interpretations. Further, throughout the individual entries, readers will find a link (http://latinamericanhistory.oxfordre.com/page/videos/) in the text to Oxford's unique *Research Encyclopedia of Latin American History*, which will take them directly to a series of hour-long video-taped interviews of prominent figures who made significant contributions to Mexico's transition to democracy politically, economically, and socially.

As has been the case for other authors in the series, I found it impossible to answer many of the questions without reiterating some of the material that appears in other answers, although I have tried to minimize such duplication.

MEXICO

WHAT EVERYONE NEEDS TO KNOW®

PART I

MAJOR ISSUES FACING
MEXICO TODAY

1

SECURITY AND VIOLENCE IN MEXICO

Why does Mexico have so much drug violence today?

Mexico's drug problems emanate from the insatiable demand for drugs in the United States. Currently, the United States serves as the largest market for drugs in the world. The level of demand by the United States rarely changes in spite of all the measures, successful and unsuccessful, that the US government has taken to prevent drugs from entering the United States. In fact, drug experts suggest that the only likely decline in drug usage in the immediate future will be among cocaine users, not because of a successful government strategy, but because baby boomers represent a disproportionate percentage of cocaine users, and their numbers are declining. The United States has spent most of its antidrug budget on an interdiction strategy, much of which has focused on the border with Mexico. During the Obama administration, increased resources were directed toward reducing demand. As part of the interdiction strategy, the United States has encouraged the Mexican government for years to prevent the shipment of drugs from and through Mexico, and to destroy drug production in Mexico. To make that strategy more effective in Mexico, the US government urged the Mexican government to expand the role of the Mexican Army, given the ineffectiveness and corruption of civilian agencies, both local and national.

When President Vicente Fox was elected in 2000, in spite of campaigning on a promise to withdraw the military from the drug war, he not only maintained the military's role but also increased its presence. He improved the effectiveness of the military through increased cooperation with the attorney general, who in his first cabinet was himself a brigadier general. The improved coordination between civil and military authorities, as well as collaboration with members of the Drug Enforcement Agency and other US officials, increased the number of drug leaders who were killed or captured. Those very successes, however, created a vacuum in the major drug cartels, leading to intense, violent confrontations among the competing cartels for control over territory and new drug routes. By the end of the Fox administration, more than thirty thousand troops were engaged in this mission.

Felipe Calderón became president in 2006. He decided to confront the drug cartels more proactively by assigning roving battalions to those communities or regions where drug-related violence was most pronounced. In the first four years of his administration, he increased the number of troops and officers from both the army and navy to slightly more than fifty thousand to perform this task, hoping to break up the large cartels into much smaller and more easily controlled units. This proactive strategy, though it resulted in the capture of more top traffickers, not only led to much higher levels of intra-cartel violence but also increased the death rate of soldiers, police, prosecutors, and innocent by-standers, contributing to a higher homicide rate, much of it drug-related. It also led to an increased level of human rights abuses by the armed forces.

President Enrique Peña Nieto, who took office in 2012, campaigned on a pledge to employ innovative strategies. He proposed a new federal force, a gendarme unit, trained in police and military skills. Originally, it was to be large enough to replace a significant percentage of the armed forces devoted to the antidrug campaign, but ultimately it totaled only five thousand members. It became active in the summer of 2014, but had no measurable effect on the drug war.

An increasing number of Mexicans, in response to the rising level of violence, now believe their personal security is compromised and that the government's strategy is largely responsible for that violence. The government's own data from the 2015 National Survey of Victimization and Perception of Public Security revealed that twenty-three million Mexicans were victims of crime in the previous year. The frequency of crime generated widespread fear of being a victim among six out of ten citizens in 2015. Drug-related homicides account for approximately a third to half of all intentional homicides, depending on how the data are calculated. The National System of Public Security released new data in 2016 indicating that homicides increased significantly in seventeen states from December 2012 through June 2016.

Has Mexico always had a drug problem?

Since Felipe Calderón became president in 2006, most of the news about Mexico published in the United States has focused on drug traffickers and the drug-related violence that has resulted from the government's intense efforts to destroy the cartels. That pattern continues to be the case under Peña Nieto. Whereas the level of drug-related violence and the large number of homicides are recent phenomena, drug trafficking has been present in Mexico for decades. Mexico's long-term drug-trafficking history is tied to the consumption of illegal products in the United States. When the United States prohibited the production and sale of alcohol in the 1920s and 1930s, Mexico and Canada both became sources of illegal shipments. The repeal of Prohibition ended the illegal transportation of alcohol across the border, but the consumption of other illegal substances grew, reflecting the huge population increase in the second half of the twentieth century. Mexico has been the source of drugs, such as marijuana, for decades and the source for the transshipments of drugs from South America. During his presidency, Richard Nixon declared a "War on Drugs," which focused US resources on an interdiction strategy to prevent drugs from coming into the United States. Under President Miguel de la Madrid (1982–88), the United States encouraged Mexico to use the army to identify drug-producing farms and to destroy their crops. To that end, battalions were sent from central Mexico to drug-producing regions in the north, including such states as Sinaloa and Chihuahua, which are currently among those most directly affected by drug cartels, where they typically spent six months each year. In the following administration, President Carlos Salinas de Gortari (1988–94) attempted to expand the military's role in the drug interdiction strategy, going beyond destroying crops to capturing drug traffickers. The army made it known that it was not amenable to such a mission, and the president withdrew his request to expand its antidrug role. As large, organized cartels seized control over trafficking and production, the United States attempted to increase its collaboration with the Mexican government and again to pressure the Mexican government to use armed forces to enhance its antidrug effort. The army accepted this expanded role in 1995, under President Ernesto Zedillo (1994–2000), and the federal government began expanding the army (its size increased 24 percent from 1994 to 2015) as well as the resources devoted to antidrug tasks. Public security expenditures increased 363 percent from 2003 to 2015, and Peña Nieto's 2014 budget proposed $4.4 billion for security, more than a third of the total federal budget. Nevertheless, by the end of the Zedillo administration, the domestic consumption of drugs had increased significantly, creating a serious social problem. As the 2011 *Addiction Survey in Mexico* reported, the percentage of Mexicans who have tried illegal drugs since 2008 has increased from 4.1 percent to 7.2 percent.

Which areas of Mexico are most affected by drug violence, who
are the primary targets, and does the violence spill across
the border?

One of the greatest misconceptions about drug-related violence
in Mexico is that all locales are equally affected. In 2010, the
Mexican government provided its first comprehensive analysis of drug-related violence based on previously classified official statistics. A review of the officially documented murders
at that time, numbering 22,700 (August 2010), revealed that 80
percent of the murders after Calderón took office (December 1,
2006) occurred in just 6 percent of Mexico's 2,456 municipalities. The report concluded that, as of that date, seven major,
violent regional conflicts among the leading drug cartels were
taking place and that 8,236 homicides (36 percent) could be
attributed to just the conflict between the Sinaloa Cartel, concentrated in northwestern Mexico along the Gulf of Cortez,
and the Juárez Cartel, located across the border from El Paso,
Texas, in Ciudad Juárez. This conflict explains why Ciudad
Juárez was ranked, at that time, as one of the most dangerous cities in the world. These two cartels were battling for control of overland routes for the transport of illegal drugs across
the Texas border, a battle won by the Sinaloa group. Further,
the Sinaloa Cartel has confronted other major cartels, including the Beltrán Leyva Organization. A recent study found
that uneven economic development among municipalities is
an important factor in explaining differing levels of violence.
Thus, deteriorating economic conditions in one's neighboring
community generate higher levels of violence in one's own
community. On a state-by-state basis in 2014, Chihuahua accounted for the highest incidence of murders, followed closely
by Guerrero, then by Sinaloa, Michoacán, Jalisco, Nuevo León,
México, and Veracruz. Only one of these states, Chihuahua,
borders the United States. Looking only at major urban populations, the Citizen Council for Public Security announced that
in 2015, among the top fifty cities worldwide with the highest

homicide rates, forty-seven were in the Western Hemisphere, ten were in Mexico, and four were in the United States. Those in Mexico were Acapulco, Culiacan, Ciudad Juárez, Ciudad Obregón, Nuevo Laredo, Ciudad Victoria, Chihuahua, Tijuana, Torreón, and Cuernavaca. Many of these cities are not located in the above-mentioned states. Surprisingly, given the drug-related homicides along the border on the Mexican side, an equal level of violence has not occurred on the northern side. One of the most interesting contrasts reinforcing this finding was the level of homicides between El Paso, Texas, and Ciudad Juárez, Chihuahua, since El Paso boasts one of the lowest homicide rates for a metropolitan area in the United States. However, drug cartel violence has spilled over in other ways, linked strongly to Mexican drug-trafficking connections throughout the United States and Canada. Murders, kidnappings, assaults, and home invasions have occurred in such diverse places as Vancouver, British Columbia; Phoenix and Tucson, Arizona; Birmingham, Alabama; Billings, Montana; and Boston, Massachusetts. The Drug Enforcement Agency identified drug distribution networks linked to the Mexican cartels in 230 cities as early as 2009.

As these figures indicate, the leading cause of drug-related deaths is homicides perpetrated by drug cartels against each other. The vast majority of victims are employed by the cartels. Indeed, the government claims that 90 percent of the victims are affiliated with the cartels. Nevertheless, public officials, police agents, members of the armed forces, journalists, and innocent bystanders have been murdered by drug traffickers. Some of these victims have been in the employ of one cartel while working against the interests of another cartel. Most, however, have been killed because they were opposed to or were investigating drug cartels and cartel ties to public officials. Such killings, some of them high profile, have expanded the impact of drug-related violence to the larger public. For example, seventy-nine mayors and former mayors were assassinated between 2006 and 2016. Of those officials, seventeen were killed in 2010, the largest figure for a single year. From 2013 to 2016, forty-one mayors were murdered. Analysts believe that some mayors who support Peña Nieto's plan to unify local police under a single state-controlled command may be especially at risk. At the beginning of 2016, only two states had implemented this strategy. Ironically, although the majority of Mexicans favored this approach, three-quarters of them had little or no confidence in the state police. Journalists are another group that has suffered a significant loss of life. One-hundred and twenty-seven journalists and media personnel were murdered from 2000 to 2014, most of them since 2006. In the first seven months of 2016, a total of nine journalists were murdered, the most in any country in the world during that period, including Syria.

According to statistics compiled by the Trans-Border Institute of the University of San Diego and the *Reforma* newspaper, drug-related homicides in Mexico have increased dramatically since President Calderón took office, but especially since 2008. During the first four years of the Fox administration (2001–4), the number of drug-related homicides remained fairly stable, ranging from 1,080 to 1,304 yearly. As Fox increased efforts to control drug cartel criminal activity, that figure increased to 1,776 in 2005 and 2,120 in 2006. In 2008, the figure increased dramatically to 6,837, in 2009 to 9,614, and by the end of 2010 it had reached an extraordinary 15,273. In 2012, some 16,800 deaths were attributed to organized crime, dropping to 11,400 in 2013 and an estimated 8,000 in 2014. Drug-related murders, as a percentage of the total number of homicides in Mexico, have also increased significantly. The homicide rate in Mexico followed a fairly consistent decline from the 1950s until 2007, which witnessed the lowest homicide rate of that decade. In 2007, depending on the source, from 26 to 31 percent of all homicides were attributable to drug-related violence, rising to 38–48 percent in 2012 and then declining to 31–39 percent in 2014. Despite the temporary decline in homicides during that brief period, it is important to stress that the incidence of other crimes increased. The government's own national survey of victims of crime in 2015 showed that at least one family member in one out of three homes reported having been a victim of crime the previous year, which represented 11 million homes and 34 million individual victims.

How are Mexico's security problems America's problems?

The most important security problem in Mexico today is the significant negative impact of organized crime and drug cartels not only in Mexico but in the rest of North America as well. Indeed, citizens believe the cartels are second only to the president in the influence they exert in Mexico. Contemporary drug cartels in Mexico are a broader reflection of organized crime. These cartels have expanded into dozens of other activities, ranging from bribery, kidnapping, and extortion, to laundering money in legal businesses, including major Mexican soccer teams. Indeed, according to the US Treasury's Office of Foreign Assets Control, 216 Mexican businesses have a direct connection to the drug trade and can be found in sixteen of Mexico's thirty-two states. To produce drugs in and to transport them through and from Mexico to the United States, the largest market for illegal substances in the world, drug cartels have increased their competition for control of the border—including illegal trafficking—as a defensive strategy against the Mexican government's aggressive posture. This has been the case since Calderón took office in 2006. Mexico's census bureau estimates that more than a hundred thousand kidnappings occur each year. More Mexicans fear being kidnapped than being victimized by any other crime. One of the concerns of Homeland Security in the United States is that terrorist groups will use drug routes, many of which are now controlled by drug-trafficking organizations (DTOs), including the Zetas—one of the seven leading DTOs—to cross surreptitiously into the United States. According to the US government, criminal organizations are generally increasing their ties to terrorist organizations. In Mexico, the only drug cartels known to have ties with a designated terrorist organization are the Revolutionary Armed Forces of Colombia (FARC) and the United Self Defense of Colombia (AUC), both of which have been tied to drug traffickers in Colombia.

Because Mexican drug cartels have to market most of their drugs in the United States, they have developed numerous links to criminal elements north of the border. One of the strongest of these connections is to juvenile gangs operating in most metropolitan areas. Cartels are also associated with gangs in major Mexican border cities, for example Ciudad Juárez, across the border from El Paso, Texas. Therefore, a concern of US law enforcement agencies is the extent to which drug cartels are financing and directing the activities of juvenile gangs in this country.

Drug cartels are also compromising dozens of government officials in the United States. Individuals working for the US government, including those in the American Embassy in Mexico City, as well as a former director of the Nogales sector of the Immigration and Naturalization Service, have been in the pay of the cartels. The cartels also support significant criminal activities in the United States beyond the illegal sale of drugs, notably money laundering and the purchase and importation of illegal weapons from the United States, largely from gun shops and shows in Texas. Billions of dollars in drug profits are shipped back on trailer trucks across the border into Mexico.

Criminal activities pose a serious threat to the sovereignty of Mexican governmental institutions on the local, state, and national levels. Drug profits are so extensive in Mexico, an estimated $25 billion to $40 billion a year, that cartels bribe governmental officials at all levels, including mayors, governors, and top federal law enforcement officials. They are also involved in financing electoral campaigns to such an extent that the National Action Party (PAN) chose its 2010 gubernatorial candidate for the border state of Tamaulipas from central party headquarters in order to prevent potentially compromised local politicians from having any undue influence. During this same campaign, a drug cartel murdered the candidate of the Institutional Revolutionary Party (PRI) shortly before the election. Officials from both parties expressed concerns about such potential criminal influences in the 2015 elections. The viability of the political leadership in Mexico at all levels, and therefore the sovereignty of governmental institutions, are at stake if these institutions cannot protect the general citizenry and reduce the high levels of perceived insecurity affecting nearly nine-tenths of the population in 2016. Eighty-seven and eighty-four percent of Mexicans considered their country and their state, respectively, to be unsafe, which, on average, has been their perception since 2010. Though they felt safest in their neighborhoods, only one-third rated them as truly safe. Such levels of insecurity related to levels of crime, real and perceived, also affect the degree of support Mexicans give to democratic governance. Therefore, the political model itself is under duress. Many analysts have argued that these perceptions had an impact on the 2012 presidential election, in which the incumbent party was ousted.

What is the origin of the drug cartels and which organizations are the major cartels?

The illegal growing of marijuana and opium poppies has a long history in Mexico. The output of both of these crops increased significantly during World War II. The US government asked Mexico to increase marijuana production for hemp and poppy production for morphine when Asian routes for these products were blocked by the Axis powers. After the war, many growers continued to produce these crops for the illegal drug market. In the 1970s and 1980s, the Mexican Army, at the request of the president, sent battalions to Sinaloa, Durango, and Chihuahua to destroy growers' fields. Today, Sinaloa and Chihuahua remain among the leading states in drug-related homicides. The United States, in response to drugs coming from South America through the Caribbean, closed down the air and sea routes, which redirected drug transshipments overland through Mexico. The existing drug-trafficking organization (DTO) in the late 1980s, led by Miguel Ángel Félix Gallardo, was responsible for developing the antecedents of many of the current cartels in Mexico, assigning different territories to individual families. These families increased their domestic production of drugs rather than merely serving as transshipment agents for the Colombian cartels. Many of the Mexican DTOs today are led by individuals who represent the third generation of traffickers in Mexico.

Currently, seven major DTOs are operating in Mexico. One is the Beltrán Leyva Organization, which established an alliance with Los Zetas, formerly a group employed by the Gulf Cartel but now on its own, emulating leading cartels. Another cartel, Knights Templar, concentrated in the state of Michoacán along the west coast of central Mexico, is involved in extortion and kidnapping, and has formed an alliance with the Beltrán Leyva Organization and Los Zetas. The Gulf Cartel, based in Matamoros, Tamaulipas, along the Texas border in the northeast corner, remains one of the leading cartels in Mexico. The Juárez Cartel in Chihuahua, which has declined in influence, has been conducting an all-out war against the Sinaloa Cartel, the largest organization, for control of drug routes through central and northwestern Mexico. The Sinaloa Cartel, often referred to as the Pacific DTO, is also fighting against the Gulf Cartel for control of its territory. The Tijuana Cartel, which also controlled routes along the Pacific Northwest, has been weakened by the loss of some of its top leaders and has largely been absorbed by the Sinaloa Cartel. The Drug Enforcement Agency reported in 2015 that at least five of Mexico's cartels (the Sinaloa Cartel, the Beltrán Leyva Organization, the Zetas, the Knights Templars, and the Gulf Cartel) have a "dominant presence" in Mexico City. These DTO alliances are fluid and change frequently as the Mexican government attempts to break them up into smaller, less powerful organizations. They often use corrupt officials to undermine the influence of their opponents while protecting themselves from security forces.

What role has Mexico played in US Northern Command?

When the United States was attacked by terrorists on September 11, 2001, one of the structural changes that came about was the creation of US Northern Command. This is a co-ordinated defense organization, located at Peterson Air Force Base in Colorado Springs, operating with the collaboration of Canada and Mexico. The rationale for such a structure in response to the global threat of terrorism was that the United States could not effectively protect its borders, and therefore its domestic security, without the assistance of its two neighbors. Despite the creation of Northern Command, Mexico refused to participate directly in the unified decision-making structure and would not send a permanent liaison officer to reside at Northern Command. Mexico's Secretariat of National Defense was willing to cooperate with the United States on certain security matters, but did not want to become involved directly or formally in a joint security organization.

The US military repeatedly asked Mexico to take an active part in Northern Command. As the United States and Mexico began to increase their collaboration in battling the drug cartels in Mexico, Mexico's level of trust toward the US military increased, especially after 2006. In Mexico, the Naval Ministry took the first step in cementing stronger relations with its counterpart in the United States. It was the first service to join the United States and other countries in joint naval exercises, suggesting that it has a more open attitude toward other countries' militaries, including that of the United States. For example, the Mexican Navy participated in the UNITAS Gold exercises in April–May 2009 and has continued to be involved in joint UNITAS exercises to the present. However, President Enrique Peña Nieto announced a historic decision in 2014 to involve the Mexican armed forces regularly in UN Peacekeeping Operations, specifically focusing on humanitarian assistance and disaster relief. Naval officers historically have been more likely than their counterparts in the army to have received advance training in the United States. In 2007, they assigned a commander to the Northern Command staff.

US Northern Command, in an attempt to broaden its relationship with other defense and security-related decision-makers in Mexico, also extended invitations to members of the Mexican Congress and to government officials with security-related responsibilities. Not to be outdone by the navy, the Mexican Army finally decided to assign its own liaison in 2009. This was the first time the Mexican Army designated a specific officer to represent its interests in a US military structure. This decision represented a significant change in attitude on the part of the Mexican military leadership. All US and Mexican military services have increased their collaboration following the implementation of the Mérida Initiative, a US congressional program designed to increase US financial assistance and war materiel in Mexico's war on drugs. This trend is demonstrated by the fact that the Pentagon has revealed that the US military participated in 150 "engagements" with Mexican troops on both sides of the border. The Congressional Research Service reported that Northern Command trained 2,959 Mexican military personnel in 2013 and 3,358 individuals in 2014. The Department of Defense contributes its own funds, overseen by Northern Command, to counter-narcotics programs, in addition to those funds provided through the Mérida Initiative. In 2015, for the first time, Northern Command announced that it and the North American Aerospace Defense Command (NORAD) would participate with the Mexican Air Force in a tactical exercise, AMALGAM EAGLE 15. The Mexican government also allowed the United States to fly drones in Mexican airspace to gather intelligence for military operations against organized crime. Ironically, drug traffickers have imitated the military by using drones for surveillance of the border, as well as transporting relatively small packages of drugs.

What do Mexicans consider to be the most important issues facing the country?

Mexicans are similar to the majority of citizens of other countries in caring most about economic and social issues that affect the quality of their daily lives. When countries are not facing unique issues, citizens are concerned about the economy and economic growth. For many decades, beginning in the 1970s, both Mexican citizens and their leaders have been concerned with the country's slow rate of growth. Despite some individual years when growth rates were strong, Mexico's economy has not kept up with the number of Mexicans who are eligible to join the workforce each year. In each of the last four presidential races—1994, 2000, 2006, and 2012—regardless of whether the economy has been performing well or not, economic issues have generally been most important to voters. In fact, on average, half of the population, or more, since 2004 has viewed the country's economic situation in a negative light (see Table 1.1).

Table 1.1 What do Mexicans consider to be their country's most important problem?

Issue	Year						
	2004 (%)	2006 (%)	2008 (%)	2010 (%)	2012 (%)	2014 (%)	Average (%)
Economic crisis	16	11	16	33	13	21	19
Inflation	3	2	4	3	2	2	3
Unemployment	25	22	17	20	12	14	19
Poverty	17	10	9	4	5	5	9
Crime	10	15	16	15	22	26	17
Drug trafficking	1	3	6	3	5	2	3
Corruption	16	7	6	4	11	9	9
Insecurity	—	11	6	6	7	7	6

Source: Courtesy of Pablo Parás, LAPOP, Vanderbilt University, 2004–14.

When Mexicans are asked what they perceive to be the most important problem their country faces, they typically rank unemployment or economic crisis first. This was true in eight out of the past ten years. Other issues of major concern include poverty, corruption, crime, and insecurity. If we lump together the leading issues related to insecurity, drug trafficking, corruption, and crime, we find that more than a third of Mexicans in the past decade considered these issues most important.

Does Mexico exercise political sovereignty throughout the republic?

In November 2008, the US Joint Forces Command of the Department of Defense issued an official report entitled *Joint Operating Environment, Challenges and Implications for the Future Joint Force*. In a section on weak and failing states, it suggested that "in terms of worst-case scenarios for the Joint Force, two large and important states bear consideration for a rapid and sudden collapse: Pakistan and Mexico." It went on to conclude that "the Mexican possibility may seem less likely, but the government, its politicians, police, and judicial infrastructure are all under sustained assault and pressure by criminal gangs and drug cartels. How that internal conflict turns out over the next several years will have a major impact on the stability of the Mexican state. Any descent by Mexico into chaos would demand an American response based on the serious implications for homeland security alone."

As can be imagined, this provocative statement, without any corroborating evidence, caused a widespread reaction in Mexico. Mexico is not nor is it bordering on being a failed state. Nevertheless, nine years after this statement was issued, to what extent does Mexico exercise control over its national territory and governance structures? (See the question on Mexico's security in this chapter.) The degree of such control is indeed a significant measure of the stability and strength of a sovereign state. According to Mexican experts, organized crime has penetrated more than three-quarters of Mexican communities. The degree to which drug cartels continue to infringe on the sovereignty of the civil governance structure in Mexico remains largely unchanged. On the local level, in various rural municipalities, drug cartels have threatened municipal leaders and police to such an extent that they no longer function independently, or they have abandoned their positions altogether. This situation encouraged 46 percent of Mexicans in 2015 to support taking personal control over enforcing the law in their communities. It also contributed to the belief among a sizable minority that organized crime does more for their local communities than does the local government. Finally, ordinary citizens currently rank drug cartels second only to state governors in exerting regional control. The conditions of such municipalities and states change over time; thus, the lack of political sovereignty is not necessarily continuous.

Moreover, if we go beyond overt control by criminal organizations and include their indirect control over political leaders and police forces, the compromising effects on political sovereignty are far more extensive, and in many cases unknown. Numerous mayors have been arrested for being in the pay of the drug cartels. Most police departments in Mexico are compromised by bribery and threats from organized crime. By 2014, Control Risks estimated that the police are involved in seven out of every ten kidnappings. Given the extent of corruption—specifically organized-crime corruption—among the police, it is impossible to protect potential witnesses who would testify against drug traffickers and their associates. Given the judicial reforms in June 2016, as a result of which judges now demand more comprehensive evidence of criminal guilt, witnesses, just as they would in the US justice system, play a critical role in the successful prosecution and conviction of criminals. In a report issued by the University of San Diego Justice in Mexico program, eight out of ten judges in 2016 agree that the reforms have had positive results. Because drug cartels are pursuing other forms of criminal activity, including the intimidation and bribery of local businesses, these activities raise the question of how much control local authorities actually exercise in their communities. The economic consequences are equally telling. As early as 2000, the estimated cost of violence to the Mexican economy was approximately 12.3 percent of the gross domestic product. In 2011, 160,000 businesses closed their doors because of organized crime. According to Coparmex, a leading employer's association, 37 percent of Mexican companies in 2014 reported being victims of extortion, corruption, kidnapping, or robbery, most notably in Guerrero, Michoacán, and Tamaulipas. Crime cost Mexican businesses 5.8 billion dollars in 2014.

2

MEXICO'S ECONOMIC DEVELOPMENT

How poor is Mexico?

The most serious problem in Mexico today is poverty. Indeed, as General Clemente Vega, President Fox's secretary of national defense once suggested, it is the number one national security problem in Mexico. There is no question that several of Mexico's other leading social and political issues are strongly linked to the extent and depth of its poverty. They include drug production and trafficking, political corruption, human rights abuses, weak social mobility, and lack of political participation. Economists traditionally measure poverty on the basis of income per capita. The World Bank has set a world standard by which countries can be compared. That standard measure of poverty is an income of less than $2 per person per day. The Bank has generated a second, more severe category, "absolute poverty," which is also defined by income. In this case the definition is $1 per person daily. Mexico's population has reached 121 million. By 2015, the poverty rate was 46.2 percent, affecting 55.3 million Mexicans. Those living in moderate poverty, 36.6 percent, totaled 43.9 million, and those in extreme poverty, 9.5 percent, reached 11.4 million.

According to those figures, when Mexico achieved an electoral democracy in 2000, approximately 50 percent of Mexicans were living in poverty, and half of those fell into the category of those living in absolute poverty. The federal government under President Zedillo (1994–2000) began seriously addressing the issue of poverty, and by the end of Vicente Fox's administration in 2006, it is estimated that Mexico had reduced poverty levels based on income to as low as 43 percent. Unfortunately, poverty figures rose again after 2008 due to the severe recession. As the analyst Miguel Székely has noted, a more sophisticated way of defining poverty is to evaluate it with respect to three variables : food, capabilities, and assets. Food poverty is measured by the monthly per capita income necessary to purchase a basic basket of food. By that standard, more than 60 percent of Mexicans were poor in the 1950s, compared with only 12 percent in 2014. Capabilities poverty is the minimum amount of money necessary to achieve acceptable levels of health or education while meeting the food poverty standard. More than 70 percent of Mexicans failed to meet the standard in the 1950s, compared with 19 percent in 2014 for education and 21 percent for health. Finally, asset poverty describes an individual who can meet the first two standards but does not earn enough for minimum levels of shelter, clothing, and transportation, a condition that described nearly 90 percent of Mexicans sixty years ago but affected 52 percent of the population in 2014. It took Mexico eighteen years, from 1994 to 2012, after a severe economic crisis in the late 1990s and then again in 2008, to bring household income back to 1992 levels. In 2014, the level of poverty increased to 53 percent, exactly the same as that in 1992.

It is important to note that poverty is distributed unevenly throughout Mexico. Seventeen million Mexicans live in rural zones, but 61 percent live in poverty, and of those, 5.2 million live in extreme poverty. Nine out of ten of those Mexicans say their work is little valued in their country. The persistent level of poverty has serious consequences for upward social mobility. Thirty-five percent of children raised in a family that ranks in the bottom fifth of the population measured by income will remain in that same category. Children raised in the top quintile of income earners will have a 60 percent chance of remaining in that category.

How is Mexico addressing its poverty?

An examination of poverty in Mexico over many years demonstrates that Mexico has been able to reduce poverty levels significantly since the mid-twentieth century. However, the government's efforts have been uneven. During the years of Mexico's so-called economic miracle, which marked a period of stable economic growth from the late 1950s to the early 1970s, poverty levels declined across all areas of measurement. In the early 1950s, the proportion of Mexicans with inadequate income to purchase basic foodstuffs was 62 percent, that of Mexicans unable to provide for education and health care was 73 percent, and that of Mexicans without adequate housing was 88 percent. By 1982, at the beginning of the Miguel de la Madrid administration, those figures had declined to 22, 30, and 53 percent, respectively. They remained stagnant for the next twelve years, showing no change until the beginning of the Ernesto Zedillo administration (1994–2000). Under Zedillo, and with the advent of the North American Free Trade Agreement (NAFTA), these measures of poverty increased significantly, generally by 15 percent or more during the first years of his administration. By 1996, however, a greater number of Mexicans began to move out of these three poverty categories. By 2005, the figures declined to slightly below 1982 levels.

The recent declines can be attributed largely to Mexican programs designed to alleviate poverty. Social expenditures by the federal government increased nearly 75 percent between 1996 and 2008. In 2015, they accounted for 59 percent of the federal budget. More important, the two major antipoverty programs of the Mexican government during those years, Progresa and Prospera (formerly Oportunidades), increased dramatically, not only in real terms, from 466 million pesos in 1997 to 38.2 billion pesos in 2008, but also as a percentage of the social budget. For example, expenditures for Prospera, a program that pays families a monthly sum for each child attending school, went from two-tenths of a percent of the social budget in 1997 to 43 percent in 2015. It is important to note that, despite Mexico's difficulties in significantly altering the level of poverty, Mexico's Human Development Index rating, reported in the 2015 UN Human Development Report, improved by 26 percent, from 1980 through 2014, on four combined measures: life expectancy at birth, expected years of schooling, mean years of schooling (which doubled), and gross national income per capita.

The Mexican government has devoted resources to Prospera because analysts from the World Bank and the Inter-American Development Bank believe that increasing the level of education is a crucial factor in lowering long-term poverty rates. Despite these efforts, variations in the level of poverty in the past three decades clearly suggest that periodic economic crises, often tied to the health of the US economy, significantly alter the distribution of income in Mexico. During most of these periods, there was little change in the distribution of income. From 1989 to 2000, the bottom 10 percent of the population earned 1.5 percent of the national income, while the top 10 percent of the population accounted for 38 percent of national income. From 2000 to 2014, the lowest group dropped to 1.1 percent in 2005, but reached 1.9 percent in 2014, the highest level since 1984. The highest income group, for the first time since 1989, declined to 34 percent in 2010 but remained at 35 percent in 2014. A significant, unintended consequence of low-income municipalities being adjacent to high-income municipalities is that violence increases in the neighboring high-income community. Despite the proven success of antipoverty programs, critics have argued for years that Mexico has done little to increase the efficiency of tax collection, thus limiting the government's ability to redistribute income through public programs. Indeed, from 2009 through 2013, the tax burden in Mexico averaged 11.5 percent of gross domestic product (GDP), the lowest in Latin America.

By 2014, it had increased to 19.7 percent of GDP, but Mexico remains the lowest-ranking country in this respect of the thirty-four members of the Organization for Economic Development and Co-operation (OECD).

What is the economic relationship between Mexico and the United States?

Mexico and the United States have had a significant economic relationship for nearly two centuries. The two most important traditional components of that relationship have been trade and direct US foreign investment in Mexico. The differences in the size of the two economies and the per capita income of the respective workforces have determined numerous aspects of the relationship. Economists describe this relationship as asymmetrical. Even though Mexico is our third-largest trading partner, and the United States is Mexico's most important trading partner, the economic impact of the United States on Mexico is far more important than that of Mexico on the United States. Any significant downturn in the US economy typically has an adverse effect on Mexico's economy, including its exports to its northern neighbor. The severe recession of 2008, with massive global consequences, was far more significant for Mexico than for other Latin American trading partners, indicated by a 20 percent drop in exports to the United States in 2009. By 2014, however, 80 percent of Mexican exports went to the United States, while 49 percent of Mexico's imports were from the United States. In 2015, Mexico purchased 16 percent of US exports.

The historic economic relationship between the two countries, as measured by direct US investment in Mexico, led Mexico to create a series of restrictions on foreign control over the economy after 1920. Those restrictions, for many decades, limited investment in Mexico because no foreigners, including US investors, were permitted to have a controlling interest in Mexican or jointly owned firms. When President Carlos Salinas

(1988–94) decided to pursue a trading block strategy for accelerating Mexican economic growth, he initially approached the European Union, not wanting to increase Mexico's dependence on the United States. In addition to negotiating a commercial treaty with the United States and Canada, the North American Free Trade Agreement (NAFTA), Salinas removed many of the restrictions on foreigners, resulting in greater investments by the United States and other countries. In 2015, Mexico received $28 billion in direct foreign investment, 53 percent of which came solely from the United States. In 2015, it became a signatory of the Trans-Pacific Partnership Agreement (TPPA), another economic trade agreement.

The asymmetrical relationship of the two economies in terms of size and income levels has led to a huge influx of immigrants from Mexico to the United States in search of jobs. Those immigrants, both legal and illegal, sent back $25 billion in 2015 (averaging $21 billion in recent years) to family members in Mexico, exceeding the income from oil revenues and contributing significantly to economic growth, especially in small communities and rural areas. Again, as a consequence of the recession, those remittance figures declined 3.6 percent in 2008 from the previous year, from a high of $26 billion for the first time since the government has kept records, and declined an additional 8 percent in 2009, for a total of only $21.3 billion. However, in 2015, they reached nearly $25 billion, which accounts for approximately 10 percent of immigrants' earnings in the United States. According to the Mexican government, remittances from relatives abroad represent close to 19 percent of total income for urban Mexican households and 27 percent for rural households.

What is the impact of NAFTA on Mexico?

President Carlos Salinas, a trained economist, believed that a positive economic future for Mexico required the country to become part of an economic bloc, making it more competitive

in world markets. Given the country's historical and disproportionate reliance on the United States for imports and exports, the president sought to link Mexico to the European
Union. Europe, facing the additional weak economies of the
recently devolved Eastern European states, demurred. Instead,
Salinas and US President George Bush collaborated on developing a North American free trade agreement with Canada,
after years of negotiation. The treaty went into effect on
January 1, 1994, the precise day of the uprising of the Zapatista
National Liberation Army (Zapatistas) against the government
in Chiapas. This uprising symbolized the resistance of indigenous peasants to the treaty.

NAFTA has exerted many types of influence on Mexico,
ranging from effects on the environment to changes in labor
rights. During the negotiating process, in anticipation of US congressional approval of the treaty, Mexican leaders responded
to pressures to make elections more plural and transparent.
Indirectly, the Mexican government's overwhelming desire to
achieve such a trade agreement moved Mexico more rapidly
along the path of democratic political development. NAFTA
negotiations also led to greater public awareness about international cooperation economically and potentially politically.
Surprising to many Mexican analysts was the fact that a majority of Mexicans, even before the approval of the treaty, viewed
the agreement, so long as it would improve their economic
situation, in a positive light. Ten years after the implementation of NAFTA, the Chicago Council on Foreign Relations did
a survey, finding that 78 percent of Mexicans thought NAFTA
was good for the US economy, compared with 44 percent who
viewed it as positive for Mexico. Fifty percent of Mexicans
considered it good for Mexican business, and nearly half assessed it as positive for creating jobs in Mexico. Two-fifths of
Mexicans believed it had improved their standard of living,
compared with 35 percent who thought that its effect had been
negative. Analysts have estimated that between one million
and two million rural jobs were lost by 2010. Mexicans were

evenly divided on the treaty's impact on the environment. In a more recent survey by the Pew Research Center, 76 percent of US respondents said they supported trade with Canada, only 52 percent favored trade with Mexico, and a third opposed NAFTA altogether.

Recent analysts agree that NAFTA dramatically increased the volume and value of trade between the two countries. A major consequence of this economic relationship has been an attempt in recent years to facilitate the shipment of goods by rail and by truck, both to and from Mexico. In fact, the first new rail link between the two countries in more than a century was initiated in 2015 with the opening of the West Rail Bypass International Bridge in Brownsville, Texas. Moreover, economists attribute increased US investment in the Mexican manufacturing sector to NAFTA. According to the Woodrow Wilson Center's Mexico Institute, such US investment means that on average, 40 percent of the components of finished Mexican products imported by the United States were manufactured in the United States. Thus, for every dollar spent on such goods from Mexico, 40 cents directly supports jobs and companies in the United States. The agreement has also altered Mexico's own labor standards so that they align more closely with international standards. During the first decade of the twenty-first century, exports accounted for one-third of Mexico's economy and half the jobs created since 1995. NAFTA set in motion the opening of the economy, and it became one of the most liberal in the world by 2012. In 2015, along with Canada and the United States, Mexico joined the Trans-Pacific Partnership, consisting of twelve countries, further broadening its reliance on economic treaties. Early assessments of the benefits to Mexico of this new agreement suggest it is risking the erosion of its privileged position in NAFTA. President Trump also issued an executive order in January 2017, withdrawing the US from the agreement. Yet, despite the positive consequences of NAFTA, Mexico's overall economic growth since its implementation has not been promising, nor has the agreement had a positive effect on income distribution. A study in 2015 concluded, "The long-run increase in manufacturing employment in Mexico (about 400,000 jobs) was small and disappointing." (For comments by one of the key policy-makers in the NAFTA agreement, see the interview with Jaime Serra Puche, secretary of commerce, 1988–1994, at latinamericanhistory.oxfordre.com/page/videos/.)

What is the State of Mexico's economy today?

Mexico is the fifteenth-largest economy in the world in gross domestic product (GDP), but ranked only 63rd in gross domestic product (GDP) per capita in 2015. In contrast, Spain is the fourteenth-largest economy based on GDP but ranks 29th in GDP per capita. From 1980 to 2000, Mexico's GDP per capita grew only 15 percent, compared with 98 percent for Chile. In terms of global competitiveness, the World Economic Forum Global Competitiveness Index has typically ranked Mexico in the bottom half of all countries since 2001. Mexico has recently improved on this ranking, placing 57th out of 133 countries in 2015 due to improvements in the efficiency of financial markets, business sophistication, and fostering innovation. However, it still ranks extremely low in level of competition (99th), rigidity of the labor market (114th), and weak institutions due to corruption's influential role. Finally, Transparency International ranks countries on perception of corruption based on market and governance conditions. Since 1999, Mexico's position among the worst countries has gone from 58th out of 99 countries surveyed to 103rd out of 175.

By 2005, Mexico had achieved a stable currency and close to a balanced budget. Yet today it faces numerous economic challenges, reflected in some of these rankings. The most important of these challenges are the country's poverty and its income inequality, a reflection of that poverty. The most difficult challenge to its future economy is a dramatically shifting demographic distribution. Currently, there are seven children younger than twenty-four for every adult aged sixty-five and older. The United Nations projects that by 2050 the number of adults older than sixty-five (20 percent of the population) will be equal to the number of Mexican children, a ratio comparable to that of the United States. Mexico must now address how to support that elderly population in the future, when those in the workforce will account for a much smaller percentage of Mexicans. It will not have the economic resources to support such a population once those ratios are altered.

Why has Mexico not been able to achieve a closer correlation between the GDP of the economy and per capita GDP? Economists have provided numerous explanations. Various studies have recommended increasing the educational levels of its population. In the past decade, for example, more than 40 percent of citizens aged twenty-five to sixty-four in Chile and Argentina received an upper secondary education (87 percent in the United States), but only 13 percent of Mexicans achieved an equivalent education. In fact, more than a quarter of this same population had not graduated from the sixth grade, an essential component of improving human capital. Mexico needs to improve education levels to stay competitive with China and India, both of which have taken numerous jobs away from Mexico in the global market. Mexico must also reform its excessive labor market regulations, which discourage new businesses and increase the costs of doing business, suggesting why the World Bank ranked Mexico so low on the flexibility of its labor market. Mexico also remains highly uncompetitive in numerous sectors of the economy. For example, two companies, Televisa and TV Azteca, continue to account for 90 percent of television programs, despite antimonopoly reforms passed in the Pact for Mexico and enacted in 2014. On the other hand, AT&T has reduced Telmex's overwhelming control over telephones, after spending $4.4 billion to acquire Lasacell and NEXTEL. It has followed up this investment with an additional $3 billion to extend cell phone service to 100 million Mexicans by 2018. Moreover, the reform legislation eliminated long-distance charges altogether. Other similarly controlled sectors include cement and bread. The number of companies on the stock market is also highly concentrated. Extended families continue to control major shares of leading companies. It is difficult to raise venture capital in Mexico and to compete in monopolized sectors. Finally, in tax revenues, Mexico ranked 136th out of 214 countries in 2014, and near the very bottom if oil revenues are excluded, making tax reform a top priority.

What kind of economic model does Mexico follow?

When Mexico created the Constitution of 1917, a reading of the provisions suggested that it would pursue a modified capitalist model in which the state was assigned a larger role in the economic lives of its citizens. The constitutional provision that specified the most direct intervention of the government in the economy defined subsoil resources, including petroleum and minerals, as belonging to all Mexicans and therefore as resources to be managed by the state. This provision ultimately led to direct government control over the oil industry after 1938, a decision that has hampered Mexico's economic expansion in the past two decades. The government has relied excessively on revenues from the oil industry to fund federal programs and has unwisely spent rather than saved them for lean years when other sources of revenue declined. The Constitution of 1917 was also revolutionary in that it included provisions for achieving a higher degree of social justice and equality. For example, it provided for a social security program long before such a program was considered by the United States. Unfortunately, Mexico was unable to implement the program until 1943.

Mexico's private sector for the remainder of the twentieth century often found itself at odds with the government, a feature of many capitalist models. But for much of this period, the incumbent party, the Institutional Revolutionary Party

(PRI), disavowed, at least publicly, the political support of the business community while carving out agrarian and labor sectors composed of government-controlled unions as two of the cornerstones of the incumbent party. In the 1970s, the federal government increased its control over numerous private sector enterprises, including restaurants and hotels, extending well beyond the traditional subsoil sectors. State control, direct and indirect, reached a high point with the nationalization of the banking and insurance industries in 1982, under President José López Portillo. It has been estimated that indirectly, by controlling the mortgages of numerous enterprises through the banks, the government, in effect, controlled approximately 85 percent of the economy.

Mexico's economic history since 1982 has been marked by neoliberal economic reforms that returned the financial institutions to private hands, decreased restrictions on foreign investment, increased trade dramatically (since 1995), and reduced state control over labor and other social actors (since 2000). Despite these and other significant changes promoting the growth and size of the private sector, certain notable features continue to characterize Mexico's capitalist economic model. Citizens' views of state versus private sector control of the economy continue to be heavily influenced by the constitutional and experiential heritage of the twentieth century. For example, in a survey completed by the Parametría polling firm in 2007, nearly three-quarters of Mexicans agreed with the statement that the government should control the economy. Only one-fifth thought the economy should be in the hands of the private sector. When asked if the private sector should increase its participation in the electric and petroleum industries, a major reform advocated by the Calderón administration, 56 percent and 55 percent, respectively, said no. In contrast, only a fourth of the population favored the change. By 2013, fully 62 percent disagreed with permitting private investment in Pemex, the government oil company. Despite overwhelming opposition of citizens to private domestic or foreign investment in the extraction of oil, Peña Nieto was able to pass constitutional reforms as part of the Pact for Mexico, to reverse the long-standing restrictions. In December 2015, as a result of this pathbreaking legislation, the government received fifty-nine bids from private companies, thirty-nine of which were Mexican firms.

An equally important feature of the private sector that extends back well before the twentieth century is the degree of control over the economy exercised by a small number of capitalist families. Of the largest one hundred companies in Mexico in 2001, forty-nine were controlled by foreigners or by the government. Of the remaining fifty-one firms, thirteen were not even listed on the stock exchange. Ninety-two percent of all sales revenues corresponded to the top one hundred companies, with the top fifty accounting for 79 percent. An analysis of thirty-four of the fifty-one domestically owned companies where adequate information was available revealed that family members controlled an absolute majority or more of the shares, in many cases as high as 60–90 percent of shares. Moreover, twenty-five of the companies' presidents or chief executive officers were family members, demonstrating an extraordinary continuity and control by leading entrepreneurial families. In 2011, of the thirty-four companies in Mexico's benchmark stock index, approximately 80 percent were controlled by individuals or families. No evidence exists to suggest these patterns have changed since these data were published.

What does the Mexican economic model teach us about development?

During the 1950s and 1960s, when Mexico experienced a long period of consistent economic growth known as the "Mexican miracle," it relied heavily on a strategy of industrialization and urban expansion. Its industrialization strategy was based heavily on a popular economic theory from that era known as "import substitution industrialization," commonly referred to as the ISI strategy and popularized by economists associated with the Economic Commission for Latin America (CEMLA), a regional organization affiliated with the United Nations. The basic premise of this strategy was that developing countries should attempt to decrease their dependency on the developed countries by expanding and diversifying their own economies through industrialization. To protect their incipient national industries against the well-established producers of similar products from the developed countries, they needed to impose tariff barriers against imports of those same products.

By the 1970s, this strategy was no longer producing high rates of economic growth. Furthermore, numerous academic studies of this period revealed that in spite of the year-to-year growth, the real income of most working-class Mexicans did not improve significantly. Furthermore, many Mexican industries were not competitive with their counterparts in other countries. It has been argued that the lack of industrial competitiveness was due in large part to the tariff barriers: they should not have remained permanently in effect, but rather reduced incrementally over time.

In 1982, a new generation of Mexican political leaders, many of whom were trained at graduate economics programs in leading US universities, exercised control over the top federal agencies that determined government macroeconomic policy. This new generation of leaders, typically referred to as "technocrats," proposed a strategy based on global competition, believing that an alignment of Mexico with a powerful trading bloc in the United States and Canada and reductions on import tariffs on goods coming from the two countries could improve the size, quality, and competitiveness of Mexican firms. This new strategy, again based on trade patterns, did increase Mexican economic growth, but as recent studies of the North American Free Trade Agreement (NAFTA) have shown, it has had little impact on the distribution of wealth and income inequality. (See question on NAFTA in this chapter.) Mexican models for the past half-century, in order to reduce poverty and income inequality, require government policies that focus specifically on antipoverty strategies, such as Prospera. The economy alone, regardless of the rate of growth, has not been able to overcome ingrained structural problems. Higher investments in elementary and secondary education, as well as in antipoverty programs, and the implementation of a progressive and more comprehensive tax structure, are complementary policies necessary to achieve the benefits of growth for all Mexicans.

Why is Mexico City so polluted and can this condition be altered?

For decades, Mexico City earned a reputation as one of the most polluted metropolitan areas in the world. In fact, the United Nations ranked it the most polluted metropolis in the world in 1992 and the most dangerous for children in 1998. By the end of the twentieth century, Mexico City's air visibility had declined from an average of 62 miles in the 1940s to only 1 mile in 2000. Ozone content exceeded safe levels on 97 percent of the days in the 1990s. How did Mexico's capital become so polluted in such a short period of time? The geography of Mexico City contributes to the man-made factors that led to this severe environmental state of affairs. The altitude of Mexico City, averaging 7,347 feet, means that the oxygen content is approximately one-fourth less than that found at sea level. Residents breathe more deeply to compensate for this oxygen differential, thus inhaling more pollutants. This "thinner" air also means that fossil fuels burn less efficiently. In addition, the metropolitan area is located in a large valley surrounded by higher mountain ranges that trap man-made pollutants. This produces what might be described as a giant bowl with an atmospheric cover.

Dramatic man-made changes exacerbated the impact of such natural climatic and geographic conditions. The city's metropolitan population increased from approximately three million in 1950 to twenty-one million by 2015. Mexicans drive four million vehicles daily, and these account for 70–80 percent of all emissions in the city. It was not until 1989 that Mexico City introduced emissions tests. These tests led to a ban on driving older cars one day a week, removing 320,000 cars weekly. On days when pollution levels are high, such cars can be banned for a second day and some manufacturing activities are eliminated. Thirty percent of Mexico's industrial output is concentrated in the metropolitan and surrounding areas. Since 1990, Mexico City's highly successful program has reduced lead levels by 95 percent, sulfur dioxide by 86 percent, and carbon monoxide by 74 percent. Mexico City established EcoBici, the largest bike-sharing program in Latin America, with four thousand bicycles and a ridership of nearly twenty million since it opened in 2010. By 2015, half a million riders a month were using this system. Participants today can be seen on the Paseo de la Reforma, the city's major downtown thoroughfare.

Recent studies suggest that to reduce air pollution further, the city should concentrate on eliminating particulates of less than 10 micrometers. For example, in 2010 a 10 percent reduction of these particulates translated into 33,000 fewer emergency room visits and 4,200 fewer hospital visits for respiratory ailments. The city's successful program has been emulated by other major metropolitan areas, but the city will have to continue to expand its efforts to further reduce deaths and illnesses attributed to air pollution.

How has Mexico addressed domestic and cross-border environmental issues?

Mexico faces numerous environmental issues internally and along the border. The major problems, regardless of location, include air pollution, hazardous waste, erosion, chemical contamination, lack of clean water, sewage treatment, and misuse of pesticides. The democratic transformation in the 1990s contributed to the development of numerous nongovernmental organizations that focus on all aspects of environmental issues, from maintaining and protecting ecological sites to eliminating air pollution. Those groups have increased public awareness of these issues, and their programs, most notably the air pollution program in Mexico City, have led to some achievements in environmental protection. In the political arena, Mexico created its own green party, the Green Ecological Party of Mexico (PVEM), which has come under the leadership of a single political family. Surveys demonstrate that Mexicans not only are aware of serious ecological threats but also support actions to eliminate global warming and other long-term national environmental issues. President Calderón made policies to reduce global warming a special and personal issue of his administration, and since leaving the presidency, he has directed the Foundation for Sustainable Development in Mexico City.

In spite of the attention that has been given to such issues, Mexico continues to face serious environmental challenges, largely because even when antipollution legislation exists, much of it is not applied and enforced. Studies also show that appropriate mechanisms for controlling economic growth in line with environmental standards were not in place in the 1990s and 2000s. The US Environmental Protection Agency (EPA), in describing the 2012 US–Mexico Border Program, referred to the air and water quality of the fourteen metropolitan areas along the border as abysmal. The reasons for these conditions include rapid demographic growth in urban centers, poorly planned development, increased waste and unavailable treatment facilities, illegal dumping, poor agricultural drainage, airborne pesticides, and degradation of natural resources. In 2015, the EPA, as part of the Border 2020 Program, awarded $521,000 to fourteen organizations in the border states to support environmental projects.

When in 1996 the United States and Mexico joined forces to address environmental issues along the border, 88 percent of households in Mexico had potable water, 69 percent were connected to sewers, and 34 percent were using sewers with wastewater treatment facilities. By 2000, those figures had already improved to 93, 75, and 75 percent, respectively. Some of these projects have been funded by the North American Development Bank. The Border 2012 Program is highlighting an improved capacity to monitor and gather data on human exposure in the border region and to improve the border infrastructure required to attack these problems. Mexico has also begun working closely with the United States since 2006 to develop sources of renewable energy that can be consumed both in Mexico and in the United States. Another priority is to increase hazardous waste facilities whose capacity is equivalent to the wastes being generated. Despite these developments, Mexico continues to face numerous challenges to improving its environmental conditions internally and along the border.

3

MEXICO'S POLITICAL DEVELOPMENT

When did Mexico become democratic?

When countries begin a process of changing from one political model to another, the transition can occur quickly or slowly and can be brought about peacefully or violently. Mexico evolved under a political model that can be described as having been semiauthoritarian from the 1920s through 2000. Most theorists use several criteria to evaluate whether or not a country has become democratic. Typically, the most important factor in almost everyone's definition of democracy is free, fair, and competitive elections. On that basis alone, it could be argued that Mexico had achieved some form of democracy, which can be labeled "electoral democracy," after the 1994 presidential election. The election itself, taking place under newly enforced electoral laws, was viewed as fair, even though some of the conditions under which the opposition parties competed against the longtime incumbent party, the Institutional Revolutionary Party (PRI), were not equitable. A more precise definition of "electoral democracy," however, suggests that a country has reached that stage when the incumbent party, which in this case had been in power for seventy-one years, loses to an opposing party, which occurred in the 2000 presidential election with the victory of the National Action Party (PAN) candidate, Vicente Fox. President Ernesto Zedillo, the victor in 1994, had contributed to an environment, built on significant electoral reforms in 1996, that ensured that the 2000 election would be fair in nearly all respects. Interestingly, it wasn't until 2016 that this definition of democracy was realized in some states where the incumbent party had never been defeated: namely, the PRI lost gubernatorial elections in four states that it had controlled since 1929: Veracruz, Tamaulipas, Quintana Roo, and Durango.

Despite these achievements, which occurred incrementally and largely without violence, Mexico should continue to be described as an electoral democracy rather than a democracy per se. Other conditions that remain to be met or are not fully implemented include the protection of human rights, a strong and equitable legal system, freedom of speech and press, transparency, and other characteristics linked to social justice. It can be said that Mexico is in the process of democratic consolidation. In other words, it has not fully embraced many of the features associated with liberal democracy in other countries. For example, although investigative journalism has increased dramatically since 2000, contributing to civic support for democratic norms and processes, journalists investigating organized crime have repeatedly been assassinated and threatened. Indeed, Mexico is one of the most dangerous countries in the world for journalists. Consequently, most reporters can no longer sign their names to stories involving serious investigations of drug cartels, nor can they carry out intensive research on drug traffickers or their links to public officials. Mexico continues to adopt other components of democracy, but it remains at the building stage to date.

How democratic is Mexico?

The answer to the preceding question as to when Mexico became democratic indicated that a number of conditions or characteristics are typically associated with a functioning democratic model. These criteria include civilian supremacy over the military, competitive elections, participation of the citizenry in the political process, a legitimate legal system, the protection of human rights, and social justice. Mexico meets only some of these criteria. It has achieved what most closely resembles a democratic political system in the competitiveness of its elections at both the local and national levels. Election results since 2000 have demonstrated the degree of competitiveness. In the 2000 presidential race, for example, the PAN defeated the longtime incumbent PRI, which came in second, and the Party of the Democratic Revolution (PRD), which came in a distant third. In 2006, the PAN was barely able to retain its control of the executive branch by defeating the second-strongest party, the PRD, by a half of 1 percent of the vote. In 2012, the PRI made a surprising comeback, winning the election with 38 percent of the vote, followed by the PRD and the PAN. Well-run elections, overseen by the National Electoral Institute and Electoral Tribunal of the Federal Judiciary in combination with public financing, have leveled the playing field for the major parties. One criticism of the electoral process was that it remained too restrictive in preventing independent candidates from running for the presidency or other elective offices. That restriction was eliminated in 2015, resulting in one independent candidate winning a gubernatorial position. Despite widespread media attention, only 0.56 percent of voters cast their ballots for independent candidates in the congressional and gubernatorial elections. In June 2016, thirteen states held elections for governor, mayor, and state legislators. Four hundred and eighty-three candidates were on the ballot, similar in number to those who ran in 2015, with 30 seeking the post of governor and 246 that of mayor. As was the case previously, few independent candidates actually won office, in spite of the fact that nine out of ten citizens expressed little or no confidence in political parties, the highest level of distrust in those institutions since 2002.

Another measure of democracy is civilian supremacy over the military. In Mexico, civilian authorities do exercise decision-making control over most aspects of the armed forces' missions, but until 2014 they continued to grant the military autonomy in arresting, trying, and convicting its own members for human rights violations against civilians. Given the number of allegations against the military for such violations, critics point out that the number of arrests and convictions is extraordinarily low. The question of ultimate civilian control over the military is associated with another important test of Mexico's democratic achievements: the protection of human rights. Since 2000, the number of alleged human rights abuses, including those committed by the armed forces, has increased significantly. The inability of the government to prevent or mitigate these abuses, and its failure to thoroughly investigate and convict civilian and military perpetrators of such abuses, extending back to Mexico's own Dirty War in the 1970s, point to Mexico's failure to meet the human rights criterion. This failure was highlighted by the disappearance of forty-three students from a teachers college in Guerrero in 2014 and the inability of the government to help locate the victims or identify the perpetrators three years later. This incident has seriously affected the confidence of elites and ordinary citizens in the Peña Nieto administration specifically, and the federal government generally, and explains partly why the president has garnered the lowest public approval rankings since 2000.

The government's tolerance of human rights abuses is also associated with the strength and functioning of Mexico's legal system. To their credit, Mexican states have implemented legal reforms that would help eliminate the widespread practice in the Mexican justice system of torturing the accused and relying exclusively on forced confessions to convict arrested suspects. Judges overwhelmingly believe these changes are positive. To date, however, these legal reforms, which were to be implemented by June 2016, have not been fully tested in practice, nor is the public convinced that they are protected under the legal system. Their perception is reinforced by the World Justice Project's 2016 report, based on eight variables related to the rule of law. The report ranks Mexico 88th out of 113 countries, among the bottom 7 countries in Latin America and the bottom 6 of all upper-middle-income countries. If Mexico is to be a democracy in the full sense of the term, it will have to achieve a reputable legal system. In the most recent Latinobarómetro survey, only 37 percent of Mexicans said they preferred democracy to other forms of government, the lowest percentage of all the Latin American countries included in the survey. Since 1995, Mexican support of a democratic model declined 12 percentage points.

Why did Mexico make the democratic transition so slowly?

When the Soviet Union collapsed and the Eastern European countries began making a transition to democracy, something similar was occurring elsewhere in the world, especially in Latin America. Most Latin American countries that had suffered under repressive, authoritarian military regimes had achieved electoral democracies by the 1980s. Yet Mexico, next door to the most influential democracy in the world, maintained its semiauthoritarian model. Mexico did not conform to the pattern found elsewhere in the region, for several important reasons.

In the first place, countries such as Brazil, Chile, and Argentina, which achieved democratic electoral status in the 1980s, were returning to an existing model of democratic politics. In Mexico, however, competitive electoral politics made only the briefest of appearances in 1911, when Francisco Madero was elected to the presidency. Therefore, few if any Mexicans in the 1980s or 1990s had any memory of, let alone personal experience with, a democratic electoral process. Second, Mexico had been ruled by an incumbent party and interchangeable elite for seven decades. The continuity and stability of the incumbent leadership contributed to the difficulty of removing the party from power through opposition politics. It also made a large number of Mexicans fearful of undergoing a change in spite of the fact that the majority of voters had become increasingly critical of the Institutional Revolutionary Party (PRI) and its leaders.

In other words, despite the leadership's numerous weaknesses, many Mexicans were afraid to try an alternative. This resistance to change became known in Mexican politics as the "fear factor." It should be remembered that in the first honest election, despite the largest turnout in Mexican history, Ernesto Zedillo, the PRI candidate, won the presidency with 49 percent of the vote, defeating the PAN candidate, who obtained 26 percent. The Catholic Church can be given partial credit for helping Mexicans overcome their fears by encouraging voters to choose whichever party they preferred and condemning any candidates who campaigned on the fear issue. In 2000, Vicente Fox won with 43 percent of the vote, defeating the PRI, which captured 33 percent of the ballots. A third of Mexican voters continued to support the party that had used a semiauthoritarian model to remain in power.

Finally, when Carlos Salinas became president in 1988, after winning a highly contested election marked by fraud, he decided to pursue a global economic strategy to improve Mexico's economic growth. He believed he could use economic success to keep his party in power while retaining most of its authoritarian features, which had been in place before 1988. Ironically, voting patterns demonstrated that those in more economically developed urban locales increasingly voted against the PRI, while the poorest, rural regions continued to support the PRI.

What can Mexico teach us about civil–military relations?

One of the political conditions that has plagued most of Latin America in the twentieth century is the involvement of the armed forces in political affairs. Most militaries in the region have taken over their respective governments at some time since the 1950s or have exercised control over civilian leadership. Mexico, however, has been a notable exception since the 1930s. After the Mexican Revolution of 1910, with the exception of Francisco Madero, Venustiano Carranza, and Emilio Portes Gil, all the presidents from 1911 to 1946 were generals who had fought in the revolution. A group of those leading veterans as well as some prominent civilians under the leadership of former president Plutarco Elias Calles, created a political organization, the National Revolutionary Party (PNR), in 1928–29, to unify the postrevolutionary leadership.

The PNR became a central vehicle for establishing a strong civilian leadership, a leadership that could compete effectively with an aging group of ambitious generals who wanted to continue wielding influence in Mexico's political process. After General Lázaro Cárdenas became president in 1934, he believed the most effective means of subordinating the army to civilian leadership was to incorporate members of the armed forces formally into the party as one of its four supporting sectors. His philosophy was that keeping the military formally involved in politics was the best way to prevent them from controlling the political system. His successor, however, and the last military president of Mexico, General Manuel Avila Camacho, reversed Cárdenas's strategy, eliminating the military sector from the party altogether, restricting military officers from direct involvement in electoral politics without permission from the secretary of national defense. Instead, selected officers were nominated for congressional and Senate seats, and a number of career officers continued to serve as governors. From a financial perspective, federal expenditures for the armed forces declined significantly over time and eventually plummeted to a percentage (of the total budget) among the bottom third of all countries. From the 1920s through the 1940s, the officer corps was professionalized through intense training at the Heroic Military College, which socialized career officers to give absolute loyalty to their superiors and to their commander in chief, the president of Mexico.

After 1946, the civilian and military leadership evolved an unwritten arrangement in which the armed forces unquestionably subordinated themselves and their missions to civilian leadership while accepting only modest increases in personnel and materiel. In exchange, the armed forces leadership was permitted to exercise considerable autonomy within its ranks, including trying its own members for legal infractions, crimes, and human rights abuses, and allocating its federal budget for specific uses within the armed forces. By sacrificing control over those decisions, civilian leaders excluded the military from the general decision-making process for the rest of the century, firmly establishing an unbroken pattern of military subordination to civilian rule.

Why has Mexico been so stable since the 1930s?

When scholars compare Mexico with all other Third World countries, one of the universal conclusions they reach is that Mexico has maintained a remarkable degree of stability for most of the twentieth century. Scholars attribute this achievement to several factors. One of these, according to many political historians, is the violent revolution the country underwent during the second decade of the twentieth century. Many Mexicans were directly affected by that violent decade or participated personally in the revolution, and their collective experiences influenced their attitudes toward political violence and peaceful political development. An entire generation of Mexicans born in the 1890s and 1900s who survived these events wanted political peace. That desire made them overly inclined to support political stability and continuity and to accept other features of the political system they found to be offensive.

Another factor was the dominance of military politicians from the late 1870s through the 1930s. After the 1920s, Mexicans favored civilian leadership. A younger generation of civilian politicians who came to power in the 1940s sacrificed the democratic political goals of the revolution, including effective suffrage, to strengthen their control over ambitious generals and other competitors and to maintain that control through the remainder of the twentieth century. This younger civilian generation also presided over a period of sustained economic growth from the 1940s through the 1960s, giving the political leadership room to maneuver and an opportunity to consolidate its control and improve its techniques for dominating the political landscape.

The most important institutional political contributor to that stability was the emergence of the National Revolutionary Party in 1929, which eventually became the Institutional Revolutionary Party (PRI). The government and party leaders were able to maintain their dominance and control over the electoral process and national leadership in all three branches of government as well as among state governors until the 1990s. Mexican political leaders affiliated with this party achieved this goal because they were pragmatic in orientation, welcomed ambitious, younger politicians from both the ideological Left and the Right, and actively recruited talented figures in secondary, preparatory, and university environments. Each generation of politicians mentored a younger generation, contributing to an incremental change in the characteristics of their personnel, while introducing new blood to each successive generation. Eventually, within its own ranks, an increasing number of politicians became disenchanted with the governing elite either because they were left out of the decision-making process or because they truly wanted a more open and decentralized process for selecting future leaders. They abandoned this incumbent coalition, effectively challenging its leaders and vying for control under the PRD and the PAN in 1988 and 1994. They finally wrested control from the incumbent leaders in the 2000 presidential election. Nevertheless, these events occurred in the electoral arena, and Mexico made the transition to electoral democracy with little violence and with continued stability.

What is the impact of the United States on Mexico's political development and democratization?

People often wonder, given the geographic proximity of Mexico to the United States, to what degree its northern neighbor influenced the pace and direction of Mexico's political development. The US government has involved itself in Mexican political affairs on numerous occasions, overtly during the Mexican–American War of 1846, the occupation of Veracruz in 1914, and the extended pursuit of Pancho Villa in northern Mexico in 1916, and through indirect pressure on Mexican foreign policy positions and its transition to democracy. For most of the second half of the twentieth century, as was true elsewhere in the region, the US government was more interested in a country's political stability than in the degree of pluralism in its politics. Until the end of the 1970s, the United States did little to encourage Mexico's leaders or its opposition critics to move in the direction of a democratic political model.

In the 1980s, when Jesse Helms was the ranking Republican on the US Senate Foreign Relations Committee, and from 1995 to 2001, when he chaired the committee, the legislative branch began using hearings under the auspices of the Subcommittee on the Western Hemisphere as a means of creating public pressure on Mexican leaders to move the country toward competitive, democratic elections. Such fair elections were first tried locally under President Miguel de la Madrid in 1983, resulting in seven major victories for the PAN in important municipalities. Their success so stunned the government that the incumbent leadership persuaded the president to return to the electoral practices of the PRI as usual. Helms's efforts were of great consequence after Carlos Salinas de Gortari was elected in a fraud-plagued race in 1988. When President Salinas joined President Bush in an effort to negotiate a three-way trade agreement among Mexico, Canada, and the United States, Helms used the Mexican government's overwhelming desire to consummate such an agreement as a means of increasing the pressure for democratic elections.

In spite of such pressure from the US legislative branch, the executive branch exercised little or no influence on Mexico's transition to democracy. If any US institutions had an impact on Mexico's political development, they were most likely a small number of influential newspapers and nongovernmental organizations (NGOs). This media, particularly the *Los Angeles Times*, the *New York Times*, the *Dallas Morning News*, and the *Wall Street Journal*, played a significant role in shaping the country's political development with its critical coverage and editorials. For example, President Salinas annulled the 1991 election results for governor of Guanajuato after a *Wall Street Journal* editorial accused them of being fraudulent; Salinas believed that the newspaper's opinion staunchly reflected that of Wall Street and that Wall Street was an essential ally in obtaining US support for NAFTA. Furthermore, the US media began publishing its own public opinion polls that, like the Mexican polls, could confirm actual voter preferences, in contrast to the returns reported by the government. NGOs in the United States collaborated closely with their counterparts in Mexico as election observers, a critical factor in forcing the Mexican government to carry out fair elections.

4

RELATIONS WITH THE UNITED STATES

What is the impact of geography on Mexico?

Mexico's proximity to the United States—the two countries share a 1,954-mile border—has had an extraordinary effect on Mexico economically, politically, and culturally. The disparity in income levels between the two countries has, had numerous consequences. Perhaps the most important of these was the influence exerted by the United States on Mexico's economic development in the nineteenth and twentieth centuries. During the reign of Porfirio Díaz, from 1884 to 1910, US investment and involvement in numerous sectors of the economy, including mining, railroads, and petroleum, allowed private actors to play an inordinate role in political and economic matters. No better example of this exists than the fact that the owners of the Cananea Consolidated Copper Co. were able to request that Arizona Rangers cross the border and come to their aid during a major strike against the company in June 1906, representing a flagrant violation of Mexican territorial sovereignty. In the twentieth century, Mexico became the United States' second most important trading partner after Canada (recently trading places back and forth with China, which achieved first place in 2015), whereas the United States remains Mexico's most important trading partner, suggesting that geographic proximity has encouraged those commercial ties. But beyond direct foreign investment—53 percent of the total by the United States in 2015—and the magnitude of the two countries' trade relations, Mexican immigration to the United States, the most significant of any country in the world, is the product of that proximity. For decades Mexicans have sought economic opportunities in the United States. In recent years, many Mexicans have sought asylum in the United States as refugees from the crime and violence in their own country. In addition to the large numbers of undocumented Mexicans who enter the United States, and the multitude of contemporary social and political issues it generates, Mexico and the United States also share the largest exchange of documented citizens in the world. It is now estimated that between 600,000 and 1 million Americans live in Mexico. (See Table 4.1 for how the geographical proximity of the United States and Mexico has affected Mexican and American views of each other.)

The proximity of the two countries historically has led to multiple conflicts, the most significant of which was the Mexican–American War of 1846, when Mexico lost much of its national territory to the United States. These historical encounters led to a strong sense of Mexican nationalism with respect to the United States. Only in recent years, reflected in the willingness of the majority of Mexicans to join in a free trade agreement with the United States if it would improve their economic situation, has Mexico tempered its nationalistic stance toward its northern neighbor. Furthermore, Mexicans have demonstrated an increased openness to more direct US involvement in security affairs, especially if they believe it will reduce the level of violence and crime in Mexico. Beyond the traditional political effects of geography on the US–Mexico relationship, the cultural consequences have been extraordinary. Given the asymmetrical nature of the relationship between the two countries and the global reach of musical, literary, artistic, and other elements of US culture, it is not surprising that Mexico too has adopted many aspects of US culture. On the other hand, in the past two decades, the cultural influence

Table 4.1 How Mexicans and Americans view each other, 2006

Statement	Mexicans (%)	Americans (%)
	Agree with the statement	
Favorable impression of Americans/ Mexicans.	35	85
Favorable impression of American/ Mexican government.	27	27
Mexicans are very hardworking.	49	53
Americans are very hardworking.	11	21
Mexicans are tolerant.	74	76
Americans are tolerant	43	79
Mexicans are law-abiding.	71	71
Americans are law-abiding.	62	91
Mexicans are racists.	49	50
Americans are racists.	73	35
Migrant workers benefit US economy.	80	67
Mexicans are discriminated against in the United States.	80	73
Democracy is more important than effective government.	63	62
"Distant neighbor" best describes how United States sees Mexico.	36	49
Which language is the best second language, English/Spanish?	89	78
Cultural impact of Mexico on United States is favorable.	40	43
Cultural impact of United States on Mexico is favorable.	21	48
Would you approve of your child marrying American/Mexican?	52	81
Community is more important than the individual.	69	72

Source: Encuesta CIDAC-ZOGBY Mexico y Estados Unidos, "Como miramos al vecino," 2006.

exerted by Mexico on the United States has grown significantly, especially in the realms of Mexican cuisine, popular music, and language. Spanish is the most widely taught language in the United States, due in no small part to Mexico's proximity and the number of American travelers to Mexico.

What has happened with immigration to the United States?

Mexican migration to the United States has a long history extending back more than a century. Immigrants have crossed the northern border for political reasons, especially during the Mexican Revolution of 1910, but typically for economic reasons, in search of a better standard of living. Today, the Mexican-born population in the United States totals nearly 11.5 million, five times as many migrants as from any other country. Of those individuals, approximately 59 percent are undocumented immigrants. As of 2013, a total of 54 million people, or 17 percent of the US population, were Hispanics. Mexicans accounted for nearly two-thirds of that figure. The dramatic increase in the Mexican-born population has occurred since World War II, and especially since the 1980s, when Mexicans went from 12 percent of the foreign-born population (41.3 million) to 28 percent in 2013. Current estimates suggest that foreign-born individuals will reach 129 million in 2060 (30 percent of the population). However, from 2009 to 2014, when 870,000 Mexicans came to the United States, 1 million actually returned to Mexico. According to BBVA Bancomer, eight out of ten Mexicans who return to their homeland end up in the informal economy, earning the equivalent of $61 a week, compared with the $245 they would earn in the United States. However, it is important to point out that the dramatic increase in drug-related violence and criminal activity since 2008 has led to an entirely different rationale for thousands of Mexicans seeking safety across the border. Statistical research, controlling for the traditional explanations for immigration from Mexico, suggests that more than a quarter million immigrants had already sought refuge in the United States by 2014 because of violence in their own country. The economic consequences of immigration are always highlighted in these discussions, but what is not well known to the US public are the political effects. Those Mexicans who live abroad become more tolerant of different religions, share less rigid political views, and become more tolerant of different sexual orientations than their compatriots at home. Furthermore, former migrants become more receptive to democratic participation and involvement in nonelectoral political activities, thus introducing and reinforcing favorable views of democracy.

Mexican immigration in the past decade has become a volatile domestic policy issue in the United States because of the size of the undocumented population, the fact that most Mexicans cross the border between the two countries illegally, and the economic impact of the largest concentration of immigrants on numerous services in local US communities, especially health and education services. The economic recession in 2008 introduced other factors, including the perception among many US workers that immigrants are taking away jobs. Symbolically and disproportionately, the perception that undocumented immigrants are a source of crime also has an impact on public opinion even if in reality federal statistics do not support this belief. The largest concentrations of Mexican immigrants can be found in California, Texas, Arizona, and Illinois, the largest of all being in Los Angeles. After 2000, undocumented immigrants could be found in increasing numbers in nearly every state until, after 2009, the outflow of immigrants from the United States began to exceed the inflow and the total number of immigrants from Mexico declined.

Most serious observers of undocumented immigration agree that immigration reform is critical. The majority of Americans also agree with the need for immigration reform. In fact, a Pew Research Center Foundation poll in 2015 found that 89 percent of Republicans and 79 percent of Democrats favored major reforms. Laws governing immigration have remained largely unchanged since the mid-1960s. President George W. Bush intended to introduce immigration reform in Congress, but his efforts were derailed by the September 11 terrorist attacks. The fundamental weakness of current immigration laws is that few individuals are able to come to the United States temporarily or permanently for work-related reasons. Statistics from Homeland Security in 2013 revealed that 66 percent of all new legal permanent residents obtained residency based on family ties, while only 16 percent did so through employment-based preferences.

Contrary to what many Americans believe, when the US economy declines, the number of Mexican immigrants also declines. Typically, critics identify the economic costs of undocumented migrants without mentioning their economic contributions. Poorly paid migrants work extensively in numerous urban services, in construction, and in the agricultural sector. The cost of vegetables, fruits, poultry, and other US food products, for example, is subsidized by the low cost of hundreds of thousands of Mexican migrant workers, documented and undocumented, who are employed in these and other important economic sectors. Mexican migrants, through economic remittances sent back to their families in Mexico exceeding $21 billion yearly since 2005, also contribute directly and significantly to the economic development of their country of origin, which in the long run will reduce migration to the United States. Remittances, which reached $25 billion in 2015, have replaced sales of oil for the first time in history as Mexico's most important source of foreign income. Western Union reports that 44 percent of the households that receive remittances are headed by women, who use these funds to cover such basic necessities as food, housing, health, and education. Remittances have also had significant social consequences. A study in 2014 reported that they reduce the number of homicides in Mexico and that an increase of 1 percent of the households receiving remittances reduces homicides by 0.04 percent. The passage of a controversial immigration bill in Arizona in 2010 was a consequence in large part of Congress's failure to address immigration reform and congressional members' failure to educate themselves and their constituencies about the complexities, both positive and negative, of undocumented immigration. Donald Trump, during the Republican presidential primary, and again during the general election, reinforced such consequences by offering brash, highly offensive comments about Mexican immigrants. In addition to proposing building a wall between the two countries, and billing Mexico for the costs, he subsequently said he would confiscate the necessary funds from these remittances. Both US Treasury officials and the director of Mexico's Federal Reserve Bank have challenged the legality and wisdom of such a policy. Since taking office, President Trump issued an executive order to build a wall between both countries despite the fact that only 42 percent of Americans supported that policy in January 2017. Interestingly, the Mexican government, in late 2015 and early 2016, perhaps in part as a response to such comments, began instructing its consular offices to encourage the 5.4 million legal immigrants who are eligible to become naturalized American citizens to apply for that status.

Could the International Boundary and Water Commission serve as an institutional model for other issues with the United States?

Many of the intractable issues facing Mexico and the United States have been on the bilateral agenda for more than half a century. One of the most difficult of these, which has received little attention in the media, in Congress, or among the general public, is the sharing of water resources, namely from the Rio Grande and Colorado Rivers, as well as the changing boundaries of the Rio Grande (Rio Bravo in Mexico). The Rio Grande extends the entire length of the Texas–Mexico border, and the Colorado flows between Baja California and Sonora, where it used to empty into the Sea of Cortez—before huge amounts of water were drawn from the river by metropolitan water districts in California, Nevada, and Arizona. Water issues, contrary to what most Americans might think, are complex and significant, and involve numerous actors—local, state, and federal. The International Boundary and Water Commission traces its history back to the second half of the nineteenth century to the establishment of the Boundary Commission in 1889. This commission was created to solve boundary issues resulting from the Rio Grande changing its course. The growth of border populations on both sides of the river in the twentieth century and the expansion of agriculture required decisions to be made about the allocation of water to both countries. Over the years, the salinity of the water increased due to repeated agricultural use in the upper regions of both rivers in the United States. This situation required complex negotiations to prevent the water from being unusable by the time it reached the lower portions of the river. At the end of World War II, in 1944, the commission was given its current name and became responsible for interpreting and applying all water treaties between the two nations. The most-well-known issue resolved by the commission was that of the El Chamizal dispute between Ciudad Juárez, Chihuahua, and El Paso, Texas, which arose when more than 600 acres of land transferred from one side to the other as a consequence of the changing river channel.

The commission is divided into two organizations on both sides of the border. These counterpart organizations consist of administrative and engineering units, and are headed by a commissioner with diplomatic status. During the past five decades they have developed an enviable, long-term relationship based on objective and meticulous technical information, resolving issues that have local, practical, and domestic consequences, efficiently and satisfactorily. As border issues increase in number and difficulty, the success of the commission offers insights into how comparable bilateral organizations might be structured and staffed to deal with environmental and other complex problems, including undocumented immigration.

What can the United States do to help Mexico?

Although there are numerous ways in which the United States could help Mexico, by far the most important assistance our country can give its southern neighbor is economic. Despite the media's intense focus on the violence in Mexico and the drug war that fuels it , Mexico's most important national security issue, both for Mexico and for the United States, is poverty. For Mexico to reduce the level of poverty and to increase the country's economic growth, it has to take numerous steps that only it alone can take. Nevertheless, the United States can help Mexico implement policies more effectively and/or enable it to redirect scarce resources to those programs that have proved most successful in addressing poverty.

The single most important contribution the United States can make to Mexico's economic development is to get its own economic house in order and to pursue a continuous, steady rate of economic growth over a long period of time. Because of the trade ties introduced by the North American Free Trade Agreement (NAFTA) in 1994, Mexico has become increasingly dependent on trade with the United States as a source of its economic growth and its foreign capital investment. A recession in the United States affects Mexico's economy more than that of any of the United States' other important trading partners.

A second policy the United States should consider adopting is to increase economic assistance to Mexico, especially by allocating funds to supplement Mexico's own efforts to reduce poverty through programs like Prospera (formerly Oportunidades). Mexico has increased its antipoverty programs since 2000, but given its limited federal revenues, the adverse effects of the 2008 recession, and the increased expenditures on national security in fighting organized crime, it needs more revenues assigned to that task. What assistance the United States does provide to Mexico has been largely security related. Furthermore, increases in Mexico's economic growth, personal income, and employment opportunities would reduce the appeal of growing plants for illegal drug use and working for organized crime.

Third, the United States could contribute significantly to Mexico's economic growth, and its ability to attract new investment, by radically reducing its demand for drugs. As President Barack Obama's drug czar indicated in an interview in 2009, if his agency received an additional $10 billion, he would spend the entire amount on drug prevention and education, not on interdiction. The violence and the economic consequences of that violence and the strength of organized crime are largely products of people's drug habits in the United States. Few investors want to risk their monies to support economic opportunities when violence is rampant and government sovereignty is in question.

Finally, the United States must take the initiative with Mexico to produce immigration reform. Mexico is losing its most creative workforce to economic opportunities in the United States. By legalizing immigration and providing documented workers temporary opportunities, the United States would also contribute to alleviating poverty in Mexico, both by employing migrants and teaching them new skills, and by providing a source of direct foreign investment through migrant remittances (see the question in this chapter on what has happened with immigration to the United States). Remittances have become the second most important source of foreign revenues after petroleum. In 2015, for the first time in Mexican economic history, remittances exceeded the revenues from petroleum. Recipients of remittances, 83 percent of which come from undocumented workers, according to the Bank of Mexico, spend nearly 80 percent of that income on housing, food, and utilities, and 7 percent on education. In 2014, remittances accounted for 1.9 percent of Mexico's gross domestic product. In the past decade, they have accounted for as much as 20 percent of the income in the poorest rural areas, exceeding the two most important cash transfer programs combined, Prospera and the agricultural support program Procampo. Finally, the Inter-American Development Bank found that every 1 percent increase in the number of households receiving remittances reduced the homicide rate by 0.05 percent.

How has Mexico influenced the United States economically?

Mexico has played a significant role in the rapid expansion of US exports in the 1990s and 2000s. Mexico has alternated between being the second and third most important trade partner of the United States in the past decade. In 2014, the United States exported a total of $240 billion worth of goods to Mexico, the most important of these products coming from the computers and electronics, transportation, petroleum, and machinery sectors. Canada purchased $312 billion of our exports in 2014. China purchased only $124 billion of US exports. Exports to Mexico accounted for approximately 1,344,000 jobs in the United States in 2014. California alone, boasting the eighth-largest economy in the world, exported more than 15 percent of its products to Mexico in 2014, exceeding what it trades with Canada, Japan, or China. As of 2014, Mexico's purchases of California exports supported nearly 200,000 jobs in the state. In fact, 17 percent of all export-supported jobs in California, which account for a fifth of all individuals employed in the state, are linked to the state's economic relationship with Mexico. More than half of those export-related positions can be traced to NAFTA. California and Texas, the two largest economies in the United States, which are two of the three largest state/ provincial economies in the world, are significantly influenced economically by Mexico. Six states in 2014—Arizona (41 percent), New Mexico (41 percent), Texas (36 percent), New Hampshire (25 percent), South Dakota (23 percent), and Nebraska (23 percent)—depended heavily on Mexico to purchase their exports. The gross domestic product (GDP) of the US and Mexican border states accounts for a fourth of the national economy of both countries combined, exceeding the GDP of all the countries in the world except for the United States, Japan, China, and Germany.

The United States provides the largest amount of direct foreign investment in Mexico, but Mexican entrepreneurs and venture capitalists invest in the United Sates. By 2013, Mexico had invested $33 billion and was the only emerging economy among the top fifteen countries with direct foreign investments in the United States. In 2015, Pemex, the government oil company, opened the first retail gasoline station in the United States, in Houston, and plans on opening four more in that city. This is a pilot project to test the American market nationally. OXXO, another Mexican firm, has opened two convenience stores in Texas and plans on investing $850 million to open nine hundred stores in the United States. Finally, Mexico also influences the US economy through tourism in the same way that US tourists play a central role in Mexico's economy. In 2014, fully seventy-five million foreigners visited the United States, generating $221 billion. Canada accounts for the largest number of visitors each year, followed by Mexico, whose seventeen million tourists in 2014 spent $19 billion. Along the border, at the end of the decade, Mexican visitors generated some $8 billion to $9 billion in sales and supported approximately 150,000 jobs.

5

MEXICO'S SOCIAL DEVELOPMENT

How inequitable is Mexican development and what are the social consequences?

Depending on the measurement used, Mexico's development is considered to be significantly inequitable; development in Latin America as a whole is marked by the greatest degree of inequality in the world. Inequality is typically measured economically, most commonly according to individuals' income levels. The most well-known economic measure is the Gini coefficient. When Mexico is compared with other middle-income economies, it ranks among those with the highest levels of inequality, along with Russia and Estonia. In income inequality, Mexico ranks about the same as the United States on the Gini scale. Some scholars have argued that other measures provide more accurate and subtle measurements of inequality. For example, to what extent is Mexico characterized by inequality in opportunity? Other combined measures of quality-of-life scales have included variables such as access to services like water and health care.

Studies by economists have shown definitively that economic inequality is linked to inequalities in water supply, drainage, and other basic structures such as housing. It also affects access to electricity, but to a lesser extent than other variables. Inequality, no matter how it is measured, affects the geography of poverty. Its effects are much more dramatic in rural than in urban areas. Indeed, the consequences of inequality in Mexico decrease significantly in urban locales. Mexico boasts some of the most developed municipalities in the world according to the United Nations Human Development Report, but at the same time it includes municipalities that are ranked lower than those found in sub-Saharan Africa. The ten lowest-ranking municipalities in a study of more than two thousand municipalities in Mexico were typically found in poor, rural states such as Oaxaca, Chiapas, and Guerrero, all of which are located in southern Mexico, a region long viewed as Mexico's poorest, while the north is recognized as the wealthiest region.

In addition to geographic inequities, which have existed for decades, economic inequities are associated with race and ethnicity. The three states just mentioned are among those with the highest percentage of indigenous Mexicans. Not only do indigenous Mexicans earn lower incomes, occupy poorer housing, and have less access to services than nonindigenous Mexicans, but they are less likely to complete elementary school, to be literate, to speak Spanish fluently, and to develop the skills necessary to improve their family's economic situation. For example, 27.2 percent of indigenous Mexicans compared with 5.4 percent of nonindigenous Mexicans are illiterate. Illiteracy rates for indigenous women are even higher, approximately 40 percent. One-third of the indigenous population is considered to be functionally illiterate. Inequality also affects trust and political participation. Social capital, the willingness of people to become involved in their societies as active citizens, is linked to social inequality and the low levels of trust in fellow citizens and institutions among those at the bottom of the economic and social ladder, as well as less empathy for crime victims. Finally, a recent study by the World Bank based on twenty years of crime statistics and inequality data from more than two thousand municipalities concluded that, from 2005 to 2010, an increment of just a point in the Gini coefficient increased drug-related homicides by ten individuals for each one hundred thousand inhabitants.

What is the current status of indigenous Mexicans?

The Mexican government recognizes sixty-two different indigenous ethnicities, accounting for 14.5 million inhabitants, approximately 12 percent of the current population. Interestingly, 26 million Mexicans in 2015 described themselves as indigenous. When Mexico achieved independence, indigenous people accounted for approximately 60 percent of all Mexicans, and by the 1900s they had declined to only 37 percent. Given Mexico's rapid demographic growth in the twentieth century, however, the absolute number of indigenous Mexicans today exceeds the total at the time of the 1910 revolution. Nearly half of indigenous people speak a native dialect, while nearly 90 percent speak both Spanish and their native language. The percentage of indigenous Mexicans who speak a native dialect varies widely depending on the language spoken. For example, Nahuatl and Maya are the most widely spoken languages, but fewer than 10 percent speak those languages exclusively. In contrast, more than a fourth of Tzeltal and Tzotzil speakers (typically from Chiapas) speak only their indigenous language. Seven out of ten indigenous Mexicans live in indigenous communities. Those states with the largest indigenous populations are Oaxaca, Chiapas, Veracruz, and Yucatán. However, those states with the highest concentration of native speakers are Chiapas, Oaxaca, and Yucatán, where they account for nearly a fourth or more of the residents, followed by Quintana Roo, Guerrero, and Hidalgo. When Mexicans described themselves as indigenous in 2015, they accounted for two-thirds of the population living in Oaxaca and Yucatán.

Indigenous people are among the poorest of all Mexicans, regardless of the measure used. In terms of income, in 2015 approximately 20 percent of Mexicans over the age of twelve living in mestizo communities had no income, compared with 31 percent who resided in predominantly indigenous municipalities. Two-fifths of Mexicans received the equivalent of, or more than, a minimum salary, compared with only one-fourth of those from indigenous communities. The average speaker of a native language had completed only four and a half years of education, while 70 percent had access to potable water, 54 percent to a sewage system, and 89 percent to electricity.

The uprising of indigenous Mexicans belonging to the Zapatista Army of National Liberation (popularly known as the Zapatistas), on January 1, 1994, focused significant attention on the plight of the indigenous population, especially in Chiapas. Also as a result of the Zapatista movement, Congress granted new rights to all indigenous communities in Mexico focusing on self-governance. The federal government recommended that the states alter their constitutions to reflect these changes, but as of 2008, only four of thirty-two states and entities had introduced such alterations. In the state of Oaxaca, 417 of the 570 municipalities use the Normative Indigenous System of selecting their leaders. This system discriminates against women, a traditional feature of the indigenous culture that was opposed by three out of four citizens in 2015. Today, when nonindigenous Mexicans are asked what word comes to mind when the term "indigenous" is mentioned, four out of ten reply "poverty," "discrimination," or "marginalization." On the other hand, nine out of ten Mexicans view their indigenous citizens in a positive light as ambassadors of ancestral Mexican culture. Consequently, Mexico has taken great pride in the architecture and achievements of their indigenous cultures, as well as in their arts and crafts, highlighted in numerous museums, including the renowned National Museum of Anthropology and History in the capital. But as many statistics reveal, native peoples in Mexico have yet to share equally in the country's social and economic development, and they remain underrepresented politically in the national leadership.

What are Mexican attitudes toward global environmental issues?

One of the dramatic shifts in global attitudes beginning in the 1990s occurred in the way people view environmental issues. Survey data from the first World Values Surveys in 1990 demonstrate this change and, more important, suggest that many countries, including Mexico, are more strongly supportive of pro-environmental policies than the United States. For example, when asked if they would give part of their income to prevent pollution, 75 percent of US respondents said yes. In contrast, 80 percent of Mexicans answered positively, placing Mexico among the top ten countries that support environmental protection, equivalent to Sweden. In the 2006 World Values Survey, only 33 percent of Americans agreed with that statement, compared with 84 percent of Mexicans (see Table 11.1). Americans ranked lower than Mexicans in their responses to the first question in 1990, 2000, and 2006. Sixty-two percent of Mexicans in 2014 indicated that, rather promoting only economic growth, they favored either protecting the environment or promoting economic growth and protecting the environment. Surprisingly, in a country with difficult economic problems and widespread poverty, more than half of all Mexicans agreed with the view that protecting the environment should be given priority over economic growth and creating jobs. That figure was equally true of low-income Mexicans, suggesting strongly entrenched views among all social classes favorable to environmental issues.

Surveys also reveal the extent to which Mexicans and others would be willing to join voluntary organizations that promote conservation and environmental protections. The United States is characterized by one of the highest levels of participation in voluntary organizations. Nine percent of Americans in the 1990s indicated they were members of an environmental organization compared with 3 percent of Mexicans. Finally, 60 percent of individuals worldwide strongly approved of ecology groups, while 70 percent of Mexicans supported such organizations, compared with only 45 percent of Americans.

Mexico has created a number of environmental organizations in the past three decades, ranging from ones that protect botanical resources to ones that work toward preventing all forms of pollution. Pronatura, founded in 1981, is by far the largest environmental group in Mexico. It is focused on protecting wildlife and wetlands, and other traditional conservation issues. It is represented in more than half of Mexico's states. Environmental issues have received a boost from former president Calderón, who has received awards for his pro-ecological activities and founded a nonprofit organization, the Sustainable Human Development Foundation, since leaving office in 2012. Yet, in spite of NGO activity and governmental regulations, Mexico is losing an estimated 0.9 percent of its forests yearly. Although public attitudes clearly favor environmental protections, most environmental laws are not enforced by the cabinet-level agency in charge of these policies, and little evidence exists of corporate or individual compliance with most environmental regulations.

PART II

HISTORICAL LEGACIES

6

MEXICO'S COLONIAL HERITAGE

How did the Spanish viceroys shape Mexico's political heritage in the nineteenth and twentieth centuries?

When Spain sent expeditions to what is today Mexico and conquered the indigenous populations, it needed to create a structure of governance for its colonies in North and South America. The Spanish Crown, through a Council of the Indies, created a system based in part on its reconquest of Spain from the Moors. The most important institution in the Spanish New World was that of the viceroy, or "vice-king." Given that Spain governed territory from the Tierra del Fuego to as far north as what is today Kansas, the task of governing posed an immense challenge because of the difficulties of communication between Spain and the New World and within the entire North American continent. For more than a century, beginning in the 1500s, Spain divided the colonies into two viceroyalties, and Mexico was part of the viceroyalty of New Spain, which eventually included the Philippine Islands.

Under the Spanish system, the viceroy exercised three major powers. He was the political leader of the entire territory encompassed by New Spain. In addition to having civil powers, he was the commander in chief of the militia in the region. Finally, he was vice-patron of the Catholic Church.

By giving the viceroy such extraordinarily broad powers, the Crown created a political institution that concentrated most decision-making authority in the hands of one individual and created a system of governance that assigned to what could be described today as the executive branch most of the political, military, and, to a great degree, religious power. This pattern of governance, marked by a weak legislative body and stronger, pluralistic local authorities, created a significant heritage during three centuries of colonial rule favoring a concentration of power in the executive branch. This, combined with the indigenous cultures' own traditions of rule by quasi-religious/political authoritarian figures, led to the imposition of an authoritarian, hierarchical form of governance on localized, semi-independent communities. The colonies remained divided into two major viceroyalties: New Spain, founded in 1535, and Peru, established in 1543. New Granada was added in 1739, and Río de la Plata in 1776.

As is the case with most authoritarian political structures, such a concentration of power creates the potential for abuses of authority, and some later viceroys, many of whom served for long terms at the whim of the Crown, were found to have been corrupt or to have abused their authority. Their behavior, combined with the concentration of authority in the viceroy, contributed in part to the colonists' growing dissatisfaction with colonial rule, eventually leading to independence movements in New Spain and elsewhere in the colonies. Nevertheless, in spite of Mexico's achieving independence in 1821, its first leader, Agustin Iturbide, declared himself emperor, continuing the authoritarian tradition established by the long reign of viceroys.

In the remainder of the nineteenth century, except for a brief period in the 1860s and 1870s, Mexico's political system was dominated by strong individual rulers, who governed through their personalities rather than through institutions, contributing to the long-term weakness of established political structures. By the twentieth century, ordinary Mexicans rejected the most durable example of this centralized control, that of Porfirio Díaz, who ruled from 1884 to 1911. Their rejection took the form of a violent revolution during the decade from 1910 to 1920. Despite the ouster of Díaz, and given a strong resolve not to allow continuous leadership, expressed by the slogan "No reelection," Mexico evolved a political system after the 1920s that relied on a centralized, authoritarian model, led by a collective leadership, but it was one in which a different president was elected every six years. Revisionist scholarship in the past decade has demonstrated that many Mexicans since independence have come to value democratic principles and have attempted to put them into practice, especially at the local level. Ironically, in spite of these significant historical events, both institutional and cultural, only one in three Mexicans today knows that Mexico earned its independence from Spain, while one in eight believes independence was gained from the United States.

What was the relationship between church and state in Mexico and why was it so different from that in the United States?

Mexico's religious heritage was quite distinct from that of the United States, which was founded on the principle of religious freedom and the separation of church and state. Beginning with the Spanish reconquest of Spain from the Moors between the 700s and the 1300s, the role of the Catholic Church as the sole representative of Christianity in Spain was essential. As recent scholarship has argued, Islam had an important impact on Spanish culture and on the intensity of its religiosity. The Spanish Crown was thus persuaded to assign the Catholic Church a fundamental role in the conquest of New Spain, a large part of which became Mexico in 1821. Beginning with expeditions to the New World, the Crown assigned two priests to every land or sea exploration. Spanish authorities believed priests could be useful in facilitating the European conquest of indigenous communities. Their belief proved to be accurate.

Indeed, a case could be made that after the initial phase of the violent conquest by soldiers, priests were essential to increasing the expansion of Spanish political authority. Using their intellectual skills, they learned numerous indigenous languages and served as liaisons among soldiers, conquistadores, and the indigenous leaders.

The Spanish authorities created an ambitious mission system, operated by members of religious orders such as the Franciscans and Jesuits and designed to produce agricultural goods and products that would benefit the Spanish economy. These missions existed throughout New Spain and eventually evolved into numerous cities in the United States, including Albuquerque, Tucson, Los Angeles, San Diego, and San Francisco. Once the colonies were established, the Church was assigned the responsibility of acting as a censor of radical ideas, including religious beliefs that were viewed as heretical to Catholicism, such as those of Judaism, Protestantism, and indigenous religions, as well as radical secular beliefs that brought into question the authority of the monarchical system on which the colonial structure relied. The Church generated an index of banned books, which were not allowed to circulate in the colonies, and controlled the publication of political and religious tracts. Church representatives served, along with civil officials, as customs inspectors, searching for such banned works on incoming ships.

Assigned these and other responsibilities, the Church, in effect, was an essential ally of the state in the New World. It supported the Crown and became an integral part of the governing structure. This does not mean, however, that the relationship between church and state did not involve tensions and conflicts. Over the centuries, for example, religious orders tried to retain long-term control over numerous mission properties, bringing them in conflict both with diocesan authorities—that is, ordinary priests—and civil authorities. They were given the responsibility of protecting the indigenous populations from exploitation by the colonists, but more typically, Church representatives colluded with the settlers to exploit the indigenous people.

What consequences did the colonial relationship between church and state have for the nineteenth and twentieth centuries?

For three centuries, the Spanish Crown and the Catholic Church collaborated in maintaining control of New Spain. Although uprisings occurred on the frontiers—for example, in Albuquerque, New Mexico—this collaboration was largely successful in maintaining order and control by civil authorities until the 1810s. After independence was achieved in 1821, Mexico began a search for a new political model to replace the Crown and the traditionally close collaboration between church and state. By the 1850s, Mexico's politically active population had evolved into two distinct ideological factions, the Liberals and the Conservatives. The Conservatives believed that in order for Mexico to develop, it needed to rely on a political model that stressed centralized authority, arguing that the Spanish authoritarian heritage, managed by Conservative politicians, would produce the best results. They thought that decentralized political authority, given Mexico's colonial heritage, was unworkable. They also believed that the Catholic Church should continue to exercise an important role in Mexico's social and political development, viewing it as an important political ally, particularly given the Church's economic wealth. It is estimated to have owned nearly half of Mexico's real estate.

By contrast, the Liberals, influenced significantly by the experience of the United States, argued that a decentralized political model, assigning greater decision-making authority to the legislative branch, was essential to Mexico's political development. They went beyond this argument, however, to suggest that the economic, social, and political influence exercised by the Catholic Church was detrimental to Mexico's development. Therefore, they wanted to destroy the Church's influence in a variety of areas. The extreme differences in the way the Conservatives and Liberals viewed the Church's role in Mexico's political future led to a civil war between the two groups. In the 1850s, after the Liberals finally defeated the Conservatives, they passed a number of laws, known as the Reform Laws, designed to permanently limit the Church's influence. These laws were incorporated into Mexico's Constitution of 1857, which remained in effect until 1917. They forced the Church to divest itself of its property and sell it on the open market. They also secularized cemeteries to prevent priests from collecting fees for performing burial services. These and other restrictions were intended to eliminate the Church's economic influence. The Liberals also believed that the Church exercised a pernicious influence on the population through its control over the educational system, which had been entirely in priests' hands. Consequently, the Liberals created a public elementary as well as a preparatory education system and eliminated Church control over schools. The conflict between church and state became a central issue in the political development of Mexico in the 1850s and 1860s, and was revived during and after the Mexican Revolution. In the 1917 Constitution, the restrictions were even more draconian: they prohibited the Church from owning real property, priests and nuns from voting, and priests and ministers from using the pulpit to express political views. The strict enforcement of such restrictions led to the Cristero Rebellion, in 1926–29, when Mexicans in support of the Church bitterly fought federal troops. Despite the removal in 1992 of certain provisions governing religious behavior in the Constitution, some of the restrictions on the role of the Catholic Church remain in effect to this day.

What is the most important heritage of Spain's economic system in Mexico?

The economic system of New Spain during the three hundred years of colonial rule influenced Mexico's political, social, and economic development in many ways during the nineteenth century and through the beginning of the twentieth. Perhaps the greatest legacy of the colonial economic tradition was the large role of the state and the weak private sector. The Crown, through the Council of the Indies and its succession of vice-roys, affected the economic and social development of hundreds of thousands of indigenous Mexicans. In assigning lands to individuals, typically from Spain, it established the preeminent role of governmental institutions in shaping the direction of economic development and favoring certain groups over others in the distribution of economic resources and favors. Similar concessions were made by President Porfirio Díaz during his 1884–1911 administration. These economic decisions reinforced the significant social distinctions between indigenous residents and the vast majority of mestizo Mexicans, on one hand, and those Mexicans solely of Spanish descent, on the other.

After independence, in the 1830s, the *peninsulares*, or Mexicans from Spain, and Creoles, Mexicans of Spanish descent born in Mexico, controlled most of the landed wealth that was not owned by the Catholic Church, which is estimated to have owned half of the real estate in Mexico in that era. The ownership of most land by a small number of Mexicans and a single corporate entity, the Church, limited the economic growth and expansion of the private sector. Most businesses employed family members in management positions, making it difficult for other Mexicans to achieve upward economic mobility on their own merits and entrepreneurial skills. Even in 2017, family control over many of Mexico's most economically influential firms continued. Those limitations have had an impact on Mexico's economic vitality and growth today,

reflected in the fact that many of the most influential corporations remain controlled by small, extended families, curtail-
ing the expansion of public ownership. The slow growth of
stock ownership among a large number of Mexicans can be
attributed in part to the weak role of the private sector after
the Mexican Revolution and the traditions that existed in the
pre-independence era.

How were social class relations determined by colonial experiences?

During the initial phase of Spanish colonization of New Spain,
few Spanish women accompanied the expeditions. Later, the
Crown encouraged wives and single women to go to the colonies, believing they were important for spreading Spanish
culture in New Spain. During the conquest of the indigenous
Mexicans, native leaders gave their daughters as prospec-
tive wives to the Spanish leaders. These two conditions led
to common-law unions throughout Mexico and altered the
demographic composition of the Spanish New World. These
unions set in motion the blending of the Spanish, the indigenous people, and the Africans brought from the Caribbean
into a mixed race known as "mestizo." The mestizo population expanded rapidly and, by the time of independence, accounted for more than half of the population. The Spaniards
devised a complex description of the racial mixtures (*castas*) of
European, indigenous, and African peoples. They eventually
created dozens of racial categories ranked by social order, from
lowest to highest.

As one might imagine, the Spaniards gave top preference to
those Mexicans who had been born in Spain. These residents
of New Spain were popularly known as *peninsulares*. The next-
highest social category comprised Mexicans of pure Spanish
descent but who were born in the New World. These individuals became known as Creoles—that is, Mexicans of European
descent. The number of *peninsulares* was quite small given

the fact that many of them represented one or two generations. The pure-blood Creoles were more numerous, but the percentage of these Creoles in the total population was still low. Further down the social ladder, the mestizos, originally consisting of Spaniards and native peoples, eventually evolved into multiple mixtures of Creole, indigenous, and African. The indigenous and African groups ranked at the very bottom of the social hierarchy. These sharp social divisions, so strongly emphasized during the colonial era, shaped social class relations in the nineteenth and twentieth centuries.

When Mexico achieved independence, the Spaniards and Creoles controlled most economic resources. Mexicans were strongly divided over the strategy they should pursue for their political and economic development, but the two leading parties, the Liberals and the Conservatives, were led and controlled largely by Creoles. It was not until the mid-nineteenth century that the mestizo class came to dominate the national political and military leadership. Despite mestizos' influence in political matters, descendants of important Creole families, owners of large landed estates and businesses, often controlled or strongly influenced political leadership at the local and state levels. The 1910 Revolution was fought in part by mestizos who wanted increased upward mobility not just in public life but also in the private sector. While indigenous Mexicans participated heavily in the revolution and their culture received symbolic recognition after 1920, for the most part their lives did not improve materially or socially, and cultural racism continued unabated.

7

THE NATIONAL PERIOD AND THE RISE OF LIBERAL–CONSERVATIVE CONFLICTS

What were the long-term consequences of Liberal–Conservative Conflicts in Mexico?

The Liberal–Conservative conflicts that emerged in Mexico after the 1830s reflect a pattern found in many other countries in South and Central America during the nineteenth century. Basically, these two parties represented opposing political and economic views as to how Mexico should be governed and how it should best pursue economic and social development. Two major ideological differences distinguished Liberals and Conservatives in Mexico, and these had serious consequences for Mexico in the twentieth century. The most important difference concerned which political model would best serve Mexico: one that concentrated power in the hands of a strong executive leader (similar to the Spanish colonial practices) or one based on the decentralization of power, reflecting the distribution of power in the evolving revolutionary American model (and in Spain shortly before independence). In theory, the Liberals favored the American and Spanish liberal models. Led by Benito Juárez, they eventually established themselves permanently in power after the defeat of a French–Conservative alliance in 1867. Juárez, according to many critics, failed to strengthen the legislative and judicial branches. Instead, he legitimized the practice of continuous leadership, a significant cause of the Mexican Revolution of 1910. When Porfirio Díaz replaced Juárez's successor by waging a rebellion, he too followed his former mentor and remained ensconced in power through seven undemocratic reelections. The revolution had been fought on the political principles of effective suffrage and "no reelection." General Álvaro Obregón, president from 1920 to 1924, following in the footsteps of Juárez and Díaz, changed the Constitution of 1917, incorporating numerous Liberal principles, and won the presidential election of 1928. He was assassinated before taking office. Revolutionary leaders led by General Plutarco Elías Calles revoked a constitutional amendment allowing reelection and created a dominant national party whose members would control the political system for the next seven decades, thus reflecting both liberal and conservative principles.

The second major ideological difference between Liberals and Conservatives had to do with their views of the Catholic Church. Unlike the Conservatives, the Liberals believed that the Church's social, economic, and political role was an impediment to Mexico's political and economic development, a view that was incorporated into the Constitution of 1857. Severe constitutional restrictions placed on the Church were not enforced during the later years of the Porfiriato, but the revolutionaries, many of whom were products of hundreds of Liberal clubs in the 1900s that wished to revive basic Liberal principles from the nineteenth century, incorporated equally harsh restrictions in the 1917 Constitution. They limited the Church's educational role, its economic influence, and its impact on politics. Some of these restrictions were eliminated in 1992 reforms to the Constitution, while others remain in effect today.

Who started the Mexican–American War and how did it affect relations with the United States?

Historians are in agreement that the US government, led by President James K. Polk, provoked Mexico into fighting a war to protect its national territory from US intervention. Polk had blatant territorial ambitions, and in 1845 the US Congress approved the annexation of the independent Republic of Texas, which Mexico still considered to be part of its national territory. Polk was not satisfied with Texas alone and wanted to buy part of New Mexico and California. The Mexicans refused his offer, and Mexican and US forces clashed briefly. Congress then declared war on Mexico on May 13, 1846. The United States invaded Mexican territory in New Mexico, California, and Texas, and occupied the port of Veracruz. General Winfield Scott led troops from Veracruz to Mexico City, taking the capital after a bitter fight in March 1847. Mexico's resistance to the US invasion is best symbolized by the deaths of six military cadets, known as Los Niños Heroes (The Child Heroes), who jumped off Chapultepec Castle rather than surrender. The United States used its occupation to force the 1848 Treaty of Guadalupe Hidalgo on Mexico, in which Mexico lost 55 percent of its national territory, including all or parts of Nevada, Colorado, Utah, California, Arizona, New Mexico, and Texas, in exchange for $15 million.

The United States' aggression toward Mexico increased Mexicans' sense of nationalism, particularly as directed toward the United States, elements of which exist to date. These historic events led to Mexico's distrust of the United States. This distrust not only has been reflected in the public posture of Mexico toward the United States in its bilateral relationship with its northern neighbor, but also can be found in concrete policy decisions. Until the 1990s, the stated national security mission of the Mexican armed forces was to defend Mexico at all costs from a US invasion. The Mexican Army's unwillingness to collaborate significantly with the US military is a consequence, in part, of this historic event. After the revolution, Mexico passed laws (directed largely at Americans) preventing foreigners from owning any property within a certain distance of its borders, as well as indirectly, through a Mexican representative, owning real estate anywhere else in Mexico. These restrictions on property ownership can be traced back to the Mexican–American War and the way in which Polk and the Democratic Party used the Texas Republic (to which Mexico had allowed heavy immigration by US settlers) to establish a foothold for the United States in its northern territories. Finally, a convincing argument can be made that Mexico lagged behind most other Latin American countries in pursuing a democratic political model in the 1980s and 1990s in part because the governing party, the Institutional Revolutionary Party (PRI), maintained a strongly nationalistic posture toward its democratic neighbor.

Who was Benito Juárez?

Sometimes referred to as "Mexico's Lincoln," Benito Juárez was the most important figure in the first two-thirds of the nineteenth century and the political father of Mexican liberalism. Benito Juárez was born in the poor southern state of Oaxaca in 1806. He was able to attend law school in Oaxaca, graduating in 1834, despite the fact that he came from humble Zapotec indigenous origins. He became a practicing lawyer and a local political leader and judge. But Conservative forces dissolved the state legislature while Juárez was serving in it. During the 1840s, the Liberals clashed violently with the Conservatives, the leading opposing political party. Juárez became governor of his home state, as a Liberal Party member, in 1847. Eventually, the Liberals defeated the Conservatives, and Juárez was appointed president of the Supreme Court in 1857, a post that made him next in line for the presidency. Shortly thereafter, the Conservatives staged a coup, eventually forcing the incumbent Liberal president to resign, and Juárez succeeded to the presidency constitutionally, leading to a civil war from 1858 to 1861 known as the War of the Reform.

During the civil conflict, the Liberals, under Juárez's leadership, issued radical reform laws that severely attacked the Catholic Church's economic and social influence and restricted the Church's ability to acquire revenues and perpetuate its economic influence through its control over real property. By 1861, the Liberals had again succeeded in defeating the Conservatives, and in March Juárez was reelected president. When his government suspended payments of its foreign debt, the French used this as an excuse to intervene and establish an empire in collaboration with the Conservatives from 1862 to 1867, placing Archduke Maximilian on the throne. Juárez led the Liberal forces against the French and Conservatives, ultimately defeating them after years of warfare. Juárez ran for the presidency in 1867, which many of his Liberal colleagues opposed, raising the issue of "no reelection." In 1871, he again ran for the presidency, but Congress decided the election, granting him the office. He died in 1872. Strongly criticized during his lifetime for his multiple reelections to the presidency and for his strengthening of presidential power, he nevertheless remained a major symbol of Mexican nationalism for his leadership against the French.

What was the War of the Reform?

In the 1830s, Liberals and Conservatives waged an ideological battle for control of Mexico's political future, which entailed constant armed conflict between the forces supporting each movement. The Liberals favored a decentralized, federalist form of government, restrictions on the social and economic influence of the Catholic Church, and economic support of small landholders. The Conservatives favored a strong, central government dominated by the executive branch, a fundamental role for the Church, indeed an alliance between church and state, and support for large manufacturing firms. The War of the Reform, sometimes referred to as the Three Years' War, took place from 1858 to 1861. It resulted from the Conservatives' reaction to the radical Liberal laws passed during the 1855–57 government of Juan N. Alvarez and Ignacio Comonfort. Historians typically refer to three notable pieces of Liberal legislation named after the cabinet ministers responsible for initiating their respective new laws, or *leyes*. The Ley Lerdo directly attacked the economic basis of the Catholic Church by forcing corporate owners, such as the Church, to sell their huge landholdings. It was passed in the hope of depriving the Church of its wealth and stimulating economic growth by making millions of acres available to the public. Unfortunately, the Liberals also applied the law to the collective holdings of indigenous communities, leading to exploitation of these communities and a loss of tribal property. The Ley Juárez, named after Benito Juárez, eliminated or restricted special legal rights that the military and the Church had retained from the colonial era. Until 2014, after a final Mexican Supreme Court decision, the armed forces could try cases involving military personnel and civilians. Finally, the Ley Iglesias introduced legislation that limited the Church's ability to charge high fees for performing Catholic sacraments, another important source of Church income.

These three laws and other radical Liberal legislation were incorporated into the 1857 Constitution. The government secularized cemeteries, removing Church control and an additional source of income. Once again, both sides gathered their forces, each controlling different geographic sections of Mexico, with the Conservatives fighting against the implementation of these laws from 1858 to 1861, and repaling them in those regions they controlled. The Liberals finally achieved political and military supremacy in 1861, defeating the Conservative armies. Juárez became president in March 1861, setting the stage for the French intervention and an alliance between the Conservatives, the Church, and the French.

Why was the Constitution of 1857 so important?

The 1857 Constitution remained in effect from 1857 to 1917, making it the most durable national legal document apart from the current 1917 Constitution. A careful reading of the 1857 Constitution clearly reveals the important political and social principles of nineteenth-century Mexico as interpreted by the Liberal Party (which eventually defeated its Conservative opponents after a series of civil wars). The 1857 Constitution had a significant impact on Mexico's political history in the late 1850s and the 1860s, after the Liberals incorporated its most radical legislation directed against the Catholic Church into the Constitution. By giving national, symbolic legitimacy to radical anti-Church beliefs, the Constitution increased Conservatives' resistance to the Liberals in the ensuing War of the Reform, 1858–61. Furthermore, in their desperation to defeat the Liberals and restore themselves and the Church and military allies to power, the Conservatives formed an ultimately disastrous alliance with the French and imposed a monarch on Mexico, a decision having important implications for Mexican nationalism and the principle of nonintervention.

The principles established in the Constitution of the United Mexican States influenced the Mexican Revolution of 1910 and the subsequent political issues that the country faced after the approval of the 1917 Constitution. The most important principles included in the Constitution were those related to the rights and structures of a federal system, sharing many similarities with the principles of the US Constitution, including freedom of speech, freedom of press, the division of power into three branches of government, the right to bear arms, and municipal autonomy, as well as uniquely Mexican provisions such as the limitation on the Church's ability to own real property and the elimination of special courts and privileges for the military and the Church.

During the administration of Porfirio Díaz, many of these political principles were ignored and abused, but the Constitution was not amended or replaced. At the turn of the century many Mexicans, opposed to the authoritarian behavior of the Díaz regime, wanted to restore in practice the basic Liberal principles found in the Constitution. They established numerous local Liberal clubs that brought together like-minded opponents of the regime. Many of these individuals became active in the revolt against Díaz and contributed significantly to political leadership during and after the revolution. The 1917 Constitution reaffirmed many of the basic political principles, restoring the original Liberal political values, while at the same time it incorporated social and economic principles (such as severe restrictions on the Catholic Church) that were far more radical than those found in the 1857 document.

Who was Porfirio Díaz and what was the Porfiriato?

Porfirio Díaz, who came from the Mexican state of Oaxaca, was born in 1830 and studied law under Benito Juárez. He left his legal studies to join the army during the Mexican–American War. Eventually he became a war hero and one of the most influential generals in the Liberal army, fighting against the Conservatives and the French intervention in the 1850s and 1860s. After the Liberals defeated the French and Conservative alliance in 1867 and his mentor Juárez became president, Díaz led a rebellion in opposition to Juárez's reelection in 1871, but he was defeated in 1872. In 1876, he led another rebellion, known as the Plan de Tuxtepec, against Juárez's successor, President Sebastián Lerdo de Tejada. He eventually defeated government forces and formally became president in 1877, but relinquished the presidency to another Liberal general, Manuel González, in 1881. He returned to the presidency in 1884 and remained in office until May 25, 1911. The formative years at the end of the nineteenth century, from 1884 to 1911, became known as the Porfiriato—that is, the period dominated by Porfirio Díaz.

The most important political aspect of Díaz's long reign was his personal control of the reins of state and his continuity in office. Like some of the long-reigning viceroys of the colonial period, Diaz acquired significant political power and authority, using this authority increasingly to dominate political decision-making. He was a skilled politician, able to

consolidate his power in many ways, including playing off political and military competitors against one another. Moreover,
he selected most of the candidates for the Mexican Congress,
sometimes running the same individual for more than one district and state. Given his long reign, Díaz's presence became
synonymous with the stability of the political system itself.

Díaz introduced or facilitated important economic changes
in the development of Mexico during this era. Among the most
important of these were foreign investment and foreign control over numerous sectors of the economy. He granted generous concessions to foreigners to develop Mexican railroads.
He believed that attracting immigrants from Europe and the
United States would help develop Mexico's vast agricultural
resources, and he offered such individuals cheap purchase
prices for large tracts of land. Rather than the kinds of farmer-
settlers who immigrated to the United States in the nineteenth
century, Mexico attracted wealthy investors who bought huge
tracts of land, complementing those large holdings already
held by influential Mexican families.

Socially, the Porfiriato became noted for enhancing social
inequalities and particularly for exploiting and repressing the
indigenous populations. For example, some of Díaz's wealthy
political allies sought to gain control of fertile lands in northwestern Mexico controlled by the Yaqui Indians. When the
Yaquis resisted, they were brutally suppressed, and hundreds
were killed and hung from telegraph poles as a lesson to their
peers. Their families were broken up, and many were shipped
to Yucatán to carry out forced labor on the henequen planta-
tions, where they died in large numbers from abuse and disease.

What were the long-term consequences of the Porfiriato for the twentieth century?

The Porfiriato, the period encompassing Porfirio Díaz's
long reign over Mexican politics (1884–1911), had numerous

long-term consequences for Mexico's political, economic, and social development into the twentieth century. Politically, the most long-lasting impact of the Porfiriato was the rejection of personalistic, authoritarian, and continuous leadership, which took many decades to evolve after Díaz was overthrown in 1911 during the revolution. The most significant political motto of the revolutionaries was "Effective Suffrage, No Reelection," in reaction to Díaz's success at keeping himself in office for decades, but it took nearly another century to implement effective suffrage. After 1920, when regular elections once again became the norm, General Álvaro Obregón did modify the no-reelection principle by amending the 1917 Constitution. Obregón was actually reelected after skipping a term, but he was assassinated before taking office. His assassination ended forever any alteration in the no-reelection principle, which became an underlying feature of contemporary Mexican politics. It was misinterpreted and applied as well to the legislative branch in 1934, although qualified by the word "consecutive." This change in the legislative electoral process weakened the legislative branch versus the executive branch. It also made legislators dependent on party members from the executive branch for nominations for decades. As part of the Pact for Mexico, the government in 2014 repealed the no-consecutive-reelection principle in the legislative branch, which will go into effect in 2018, allowing congressional deputies to be reelected three times and senators once; surprisingly, mayors, the only elected executive officials, will be allowed to serve two terms. Most analysts consider the no-reelection principle to be a serious impediment to the balance of power between the branches of government. Nevertheless, after 1920, the postrevolutionary elite succeeded in creating a party that enabled them to maintain control over the presidency.

Economically and socially, the failures and prejudices of the Porfiriato resulted in some unique principles being incorporated in the 1917 Constitution. The Constitution legitimized a mixed economic model of state capitalism. The state took on a larger role after 1920, ostensibly to protect and increase economic benefits for working-class Mexicans. The actual benefits were limited, even though organized labor became a major political supporter of the postrevolutionary party and its leaders. The state placed subsoil resources, such as valuable minerals and oil, in the hands of the nation, to be administered by the state, so all Mexicans would become economic beneficiaries. This was a response to the wealthy concessionaries who received valuable property at bargain prices from the Díaz administration. In 2015, for the first time since the nationalization of petroleum companies in 1938, private and foreign domestic investors were allowed to bid on oil leases.

Socially, the racial prejudices encouraged by the Porfiriato generated a reaction among Liberals who favored policies promoting the dignity of the individual and greater social equality. For example, the postrevolutionary government declared its intention to provide free public education to all Mexicans through elementary school. Under the leadership of several notable secretaries of public education in the 1920s and 1930s, efforts were made to implement these educational goals embedded in the 1917 Constitution, but the government fell far short of fulfilling them, many of which were put in place in reaction to the Porfiriato's failures.

8

THE MEXICAN REVOLUTION AND A NEW POLITICAL MODEL FOR MEXICO

THE MEXICAN REVOLUTION

What were the causes of the Mexican Revolution of 1910?

Historians have argued for a century about which were the most important causes of the Mexican Revolution. Although they do not agree on their relative importance, they do agree on what the fundamental causes of the revolution were. The weight given to each causal factor varies according to the geographic region and social class of a given group of revolutionaries. Nonetheless, the underlying causes of the revolution are reflected in articles of the 1917 Constitution.

Many of the Mexicans who lived in northern Mexico and participated in the revolution did so due to their experiences with foreigners who owned mines, large properties, and railroads. Working-class Mexicans employed by foreign-owned companies typically viewed themselves as second-class citizens. For example, those who worked for the railroads were not given skilled engineering positions but instead were assigned to unskilled positions. One of the goals of mining engineers graduating from the National School of Engineering as late as the 1940s was to occupy all of the professional engineering positions in every foreign-owned mine in Mexico. This antiforeign sentiment is reflected in the fact that the Constitution assigned subsoil rights to the nation, rather than viewing them as private property.

A second cause of the revolution, from the viewpoint of working Mexicans, was the lack of labor rights. During the Porfiriato, from 1884 to 1911, although Díaz occasionally permitted and even mediated peaceful strikes, negotiating with moderate labor leaders, his administration was renowned for suppressing labor strikes, particularly during the last decade of his administration. Two such occurrences included the Cananea mining demonstration in Sonora in 1906, when Arizona Rangers crossed the border as strikebreakers, and the notorious Río Blanco Mill strike in Puebla in 1909, during which dozens of workers lost their lives. These and other labor activities and strikes led to numerous demands for improved working conditions for all Mexicans; these demands included a limit on the number of hours workers could be required to put in each day, a minimum percentage of Mexican workers in foreign-owned plants, and minimum wages. The most important revolutionary demand, which became Article 123 of the Constitution, was that labor be granted the legal right to strike. For rural workers, both mestizo and indigenous, who were typically exploited to an even greater extent than their urban counterparts, the revolution meant the redistribution of land to peasants who wanted their own farms. Land was a central issue for the men and women who supported Emiliano Zapata, a leader who emerged from Morelos. Such abuses as debt servitude and company stores (owned by the landowner), which monopolized workers' access to necessary goods, were also prohibited in the revolutionary articles incorporated in the Constitution.

Additionally, middle-class Mexicans, professionals, and intellectuals were strongly interested in political change, either because they favored a democratic polity or because they harbored political ambitions themselves and hoped for more upward political mobility as a consequence of civil violence. The most important political principles, advocated strongly by Francisco I. Madero, who had opposed Díaz in the 1910 presidential election, were effective suffrage and a ban on continuous leadership, referred to as "no reelection." The phrase "Effective Suffrage, No Reelection" appeared at the bottom of every piece of official correspondence from the federal government until well into the 1970s, indicative of its symbolic importance for postrevolutionary leaders. Many politicized Mexicans also wanted municipal autonomy, having experienced the intervention of authoritarian state or federal entities.

Who was Francisco I. Madero?

Francisco Madero, born in 1873, was a wealthy landowner from Coahuila, a northern border state below Texas. The son of a prominent industrialist and businessman, he and many of his relatives opposed Díaz's authoritarian regime. Madero was not a radical revolutionary but an individual with a social conscience who wanted to change how Mexico was led politically and the direction it pursued socially. He treated his own employees humanely, providing them with health benefits, access to schools for their children, and adequate salaries. In 1905, he began his anti-reelectionist activities and founded the Benito Juárez Anti-Reelectionist Club to oppose Porfirio Díaz's continued reelection as president. In 1908, he published an influential book titled *The Presidential Succession of 1910*, in which he laid out some of his basic principles and criticized the president for his antidemocratic practices. That same year, President Díaz, in an interview with a US journalist, made the statement that the 1910 election would be democratic, opening the door for an opposition candidate. Madero took him at his word and eventually became the candidate of the Anti-Reelectionist Party, running on the motto "Effective Suffrage, No Reelection." He conducted a national campaign, but in the final stages he was arrested and imprisoned in San Luis Potosí. Díaz declared himself the winner in a fraudulent election.

Madero was able to escape to San Antonio, Texas, where he issued his celebrated Plan of San Luis Potosi, which contains many of his prominent principles.

Madero ultimately returned to Mexico in 1911 and led a revolution in the northern states. Using a victory over the federal army in Ciudad Juárez led by Pancho Villa and Pascual Orozco as leverage, he forced Díaz and his vice president to resign in May 1911. Madero did not seize the presidency; instead he allowed an interim president to be installed, while he ran for and won the presidency in a new election in late 1911, taking office in November. Madero and his vice president, José María Pino Suárez, governed for two years, during which time he faced considerable opposition from former supporters of Díaz, as well as from more radical revolutionaries, such as Emiliano Zapata, who were interested in land reform and other socially radical policies. Madero did not provide the strong leadership necessary to weaken his political enemies, who—led by General Victoriano Huerta, a career federal officer under Díaz—overthrew Madero and murdered both him and his vice president on February 18, 1913. Madero's murder provided the catalyst for the truly violent and radical phase of the Mexican Revolution, the years 1913 to 1916. This period saw the birth of the major revolutionary principles found in the 1917 Constitution, as well as the violence that would pervade the country until 1920 and beyond. The US ambassador's complicity in Madero's overthrow and murder also contributed significantly to Mexicans' nationalistic posture toward and distrust of the United States.

Who really was Pancho Villa?

Born (José) Doroteo Arango (Arámbula) in 1878, Pancho (Francisco) Villa was the son of poor peasants who worked on one of the largest landholdings in the state of Durango. He helped support his brothers and sister when his father died, eventually becoming a member of a bandit gang, after which he left the state in 1902 and settled in Chihuahua. He continued his illegal activities and joined Pascual Orozco, with others whom he recruited, in a revolt against Díaz in 1911. Villa participated in the victorious attack on Ciudad Juárez, which gave Madero a decisive victory over federal troops and the ability to force Díaz to resign. Later, President Madero saved Villa from a firing squad, after which Villa escaped from prison. When General Victoriano Huerta led a military coup against Madero and had him murdered in 1913, he also killed Abraham González, a friend of Villa's, who originally recruited Villa to Madero's cause in 1910. Villa gathered up a force of supporters and declared his support for the Constitutionalist Army led by Venustiano Carranza. This army was composed of Mexicans who wanted to restore constitutional government and defeat the reactionary forces aligned with Huerta. Briefly provisional governor of Chihuahua in 1913–14, Villa implemented radical policies in seizing property from large landholders and converting numerous privately owned buildings into schools.

Villa was very popular in Chihuahua and was able to persuade a large number of men to join his army. He seized cattle and traded it for arms across the border in the United States. He became one of the most effective generals in the Constitutionalist Army. As the leader of the Division of the North. Villa commandeered trains to carry his cavalry. He used the railroad system to create a highly mobile force. In 1914, he defeated the federal army in the Battle of Zacatecas, a decisive victory in ousting Huerta. The victorious generals joined together in the Convention of Aguascalientes, proposing some radical solutions to Mexico's economic and social problems, but their views were opposed by Carranza. Villa, Emiliano Zapata, and others chose to oppose Carranza and his allies, most notably General Álvaro Obregón, thus initiating another phase of the civil war from 1914 to 1916. Villa and his army were ultimately defeated by Obregón in the Battle of Celaya (1915), with Obregón using modern battle techniques developed for World War I, including the deployment of a "military aviation arm" to destroy Villa's cavalry charges. Villa, who lost the support of the United States and was deprived of access to additional weapons, sent his troops across the border to attack the US Cavalry garrison at Columbus, New Mexico, on March 9, 1916. This attack led to the Pershing Expedition, headed by General John "Black Jack" Pershing, who unsuccessfully pursued Villa's forces into northern Mexico. Unable to defeat Carranza's troops, Villa eventually settled for a large ranch from the government for his men and their families, but he was assassinated in 1923, with the complicity of government officials. Today, he remains a major figure in Mexican popular culture.

Who benefited most from the Mexican Revolution?

Historians have never fully agreed whether Mexico underwent a truly social revolution. Regardless of the depth or definition of its revolution, the cost in human lives and the destruction of property was devastating. The Mexican Revolution, like most significant revolutions in other countries, went through a series of phases between 1910 and 1920. The incumbent regime was easily eliminated without much bloodshed by 1911, but the initial, moderate victors who governed from 1911 to 1913 were removed violently by a counterrevolution. That counterrevolution produced the first truly violent phase of the revolution, won by the revolutionaries in 1914. But the revolutionaries themselves, again similar to those in other historic revolutions, including that of the Soviet Union, had a falling out over the path the revolution should take. Essentially, those favoring more radical solutions to the maldistribution of land and other social and economic ills were defeated by those revolutionaries who favored more modest reforms. The moderates, under Venustiano Carranza, took control of the government in 1916. But at the end of the decade, General Álvaro Obregón, Carranza's leading general in defeating the more radical revolutionary forces, wanted to pursue more socially reformist policies, placing himself ideologically somewhere between Carranza and the revolutionaries he himself had defeated in 1914–15.

An examination of the beneficiaries of the Mexican Revolution makes clear that those who fared the best politically were members of the rising middle class. Generally speaking, these individuals, who held political posts after 1920, were members of an educated, professional class, most of whom had not actively participated in the revolution. The most adversely affected individuals were Mexicans from wealthy entrepreneurial and landholding families, whose representation in the political class was nearly eliminated. Those Mexicans who had fought in the revolution, typically coming from modest, working-class rural families, dominated the leadership during the revolutionary years, especially from 1914 to 1920, but not during the institutionalized postrevolutionary period. Except for the revolutionary generals who became presidents for most of the period from 1920 to 1946, the majority of national figures were civilians. It took numerous decades after 1920 before the standard of living of large groups of poorer Mexicans improved. This improvement occurred typically during the 1950s and 1960s, which witnessed the largest increase in the size of the middle class and the longest era of economic growth, and therefore resulted in a concomitant decrease in the percentage of Mexicans falling into the working class.

Could Mexico have achieved changes in its structures through peaceful means instead of violence?

Historians and citizens alike, when evaluating the consequences of civil wars and violent revolutions, often wonder in retrospect if structural change could have occurred through peaceful rather than violent means, avoiding the great losses of life and the accompanying physical destruction. To what extent did Mexico alter its political and economic structures after 1920? Politically, it is possible to measure some significant changes in the composition and patterns of leadership that were brought about by the revolution. For example, recent research empirically demonstrates that for a brief period, especially in the 1920s and 1930s, ambitious Mexicans of modest, working-class backgrounds and from small provincial communities and villages gained access to national political office and state governorships. Such Mexicans in leadership positions never came close to representing the percentage of all Mexicans from these socioeconomic circumstances; nevertheless, they represented the highest percentage of such Mexicans to achieve important political office before or since.

One of the credentials most useful for achieving upward political mobility before the revolution was a college degree. Certain public universities and preparatory schools played a significant role in turning out future political leaders. Mexico produced a remarkably large number of college-educated politicians prior to 1911. After 1920, however, college degrees were not valued to the same degree as before the revolution, and it took decades before prominent political figures achieved educational levels equal to those of their prerevolutionary peers.

It is more difficult to measure the structural economic changes wrought by the revolution. Many historians are not in agreement with the idea that Mexico underwent a "true" social revolution, because they do not find adequate evidence of major economic changes. Most historians agree that these would include changes in landownership. There is no question that under some presidential administrations, the Mexican government began to distribute land to landless peasants as early as 1915. Eventually, the largest amounts of land were distributed to farmers through the *ejido* system, a land tenure system based on the indigenous principle of assigning land to villages collectively. To each resident who wanted to farm, this system granted rights to use the land and to pass the land on to their children, but not to pass on an actual deed to the land. The government continued to give out land for most of the twentieth century, breaking up most of the large landholdings in Mexico. While millions of peasants obtained their own land, the government never provided adequate credit to make these farms productive, nor in many cases did it distribute enough land to make earning a living feasible. Peasants could not borrow from private banks because they did not own the land. By the 1960s, most of the *ejido* properties were being illegally rented and consolidated into larger farms. Thus, the argument can be made that the revolution produced a more equitable redistribution of land, but at the same time did little to improve the actual economic welfare of the recipients.

How did the revolution alter political institutions and civil–military relations?

If we examine the political development and institutional relationships following the revolution in the 1920s and 1930s, it becomes clear that the foundations for the political relationships that characterized Mexico for the next century can be traced to that period. It is essential to note that the Mexicans who succeeded in taking control of the political process after 1920, with few exceptions, were part of the revolutionary forces that determined the outcome of the decade of violence from 1910 to 1920. The senior generals became the presidents, the secretaries of national defense, the provincial zone commanders, and often the governors during the next two decades. Because these generals were the product of a popular army, in effect multiple guerrilla movements, they had to institutionalize the officer corps and gradually eliminate a large number of veterans from active duty. The leadership established a new military school, which became the Heroic Military College, in the 1920s. It developed an authoritarian and strict curriculum focused on obedience to one's superior officer and to the president. This was a remarkable achievement because declining portions of the existing popular army revolted, without success, against the government in 1923, 1927, and 1929.

The revolutionary generals, under the leadership of former president Plutarco Elías Calles and after the assassination of President-elect Álvaro Obregón in 1928, decided to create a political organization, the National Revolutionary Party, to co-opt politically ambitious individuals, military and civilian alike, and create a substitute for personalistic leadership. It is clear that while Calles initiated this concept to further his own personal political ambitions, he unintentionally provided a structure for a circulating, collective elite that emerged from the revolutionary era. President Lázaro Cárdenas, one of the last revolutionary generals to govern Mexico, added several additional features that strengthened the control of civilian actors, while concentrating more influence in the executive branch. He formalized four sectors in the party, creating a corporatist system in which occupational groups would be represented in the party organization and in Congress. He established unions and business organizations to channel those groups' demands to the government. To strengthen his own position as president and eliminate his subordination to his former mentor, General Calles, Cárdenas altered the Constitution to prevent members of the lower chamber of Congress from being consecutively reelected, a policy which remained in effect until 2018. This weakened Congress while strengthening executive power over the nominees for congressional seats. Although numerous other political principles emerged from the revolutionary era, the principles of military subordination to civilian control and a strong, unified political organization controlled by a dominant executive branch determined many aspects of the political process until 2000.

What was the attitude of the United States toward the revolution?

The United States had maintained good relations with Porfirio Díaz prior to the opening days of the revolution in 1910.

In fact, the activities of the US government on behalf of Mexico in the decade immediately preceding the revolution are indicative of a collaborative relationship between the two countries. The United States helped the Díaz government persecute some of the more radical anti-Díaz figures in the labor movement, the most notable example of which were the Flores Magón brothers, who were significant precursors of the revolution. Ricardo and Enrique Flores Magón were forced into exile in San Antonio, Texas, where they were able to publish their antiregime newspaper, *Regeneración*, one of the most influential publications in converting Mexicans to the revolutionary cause. They were forced to move to St. Louis, which hosted a large exile community of pro-revolutionaries, but there they were also harassed by police, and some supporters were imprisoned. Ricardo was arrested in 1907, and tried and imprisoned in Arizona from 1909 to 1910. Other revolutionaries fared better. Pancho Villa, for example, cultivated contacts along the Texas border, including US Army commanders. Authorities winked at his exchange of cattle for weapons during the early years of the revolution. Francisco Madero, who opposed Díaz in the 1910 election and eventually fled to the United States, was viewed as a moderate by the US government and business community and therefore as a viable replacement for Díaz.

When Francisco Madero became president, Henry Lane Wilson, the US ambassador, interfered repeatedly in Mexican affairs, attempting to undercut the president's legitimacy. Most tragically, he colluded with General Victoriano Huerta to remove Madero by force, ultimately leading to the murder of the president and the vice president by the usurpers. President Woodrow Wilson came to office in 1914 and resisted Ambassador Wilson's recommendation to recognize the Huerta regime. He removed Wilson and decided to provide aid to the Constitutionalist Army opposing the regime. But using an incident involving the US Navy in the port of Veracruz, President Wilson ordered the occupation of the port by US forces. Mexicans from all over the republic responded to this blatant intervention, organizing groups of volunteers, including students, to travel to Veracruz to oppose the United States' actions.

When Huerta was finally ousted by Constitutionalists and the victorious revolutionaries embarked on another violent phase of the revolution, the United States intervened once again. This time it chased Villa's troops after they crossed the border and attacked Columbus, New Mexico, in March 1916. Ultimately, the US government chose to recognize Venustiano Carranza's administration. Regardless of its motivations or the individual factions it supported from 1911 to 1920, the United States pursued an actively interventionist agenda in Mexico, including a range of strategies from the use of force to financial support.

What is the Constitution of 1917?

In order to understand Mexico's development throughout most of the twentieth century and many of its current policies, it is essential to understand the most important articles of the 1917 Constitution. The 1917 Constitution, currently in effect, emerged from the violent confrontations during the revolutionary decade, especially from those events occurring during 1911–16. Mexico held a special constitutional convention, electing representatives from every state. Many of these individuals advocated an ideological posture reflecting the major social, economic, and political goals of the revolution, a posture that was far more radical than the beliefs subscribed to by the 1916–20 government of Venustiano Carranza. The 1917 Constitution became an essential component of the rhetoric of the Mexican Revolution, legitimizing numerous concepts for the Mexican public, who developed a reverence for its basic principles.

It can be argued that one of the principles that emerged from the revolutionary era represented symbolically by this document is constitutionalism. Expressed differently, the fundamental principles contained in the Constitution have achieved a legitimacy in the eyes of most Mexicans that exceeds their legal status. The influence of constitutionalism in the popular culture can be illustrated by the fact that in various cities in Mexico, including the national capital, streets are named after the most important individual articles, not just the word "constitution," a common practice in older US towns and villages. For example, in Tijuana, there is an arch known as Calle Articulo 123, which is located near Revolución and First Street, not far from Constitución. Articles 3, 27, and 130 are also the names of important streets in major cities and state capitals.

If one had to summarize the most important principles found in these four articles, one could refer to the most significant causes of the Mexican Revolution. Article 3, which is devoted to education, requires that the government ensure that education at the elementary, secondary, and normal levels is free of religious influence; that elementary education is compulsory and free; and that education promotes the dignity of the individual and equal rights. Article 27 focuses on ownership of land and water, and the need to divide large landed estates and develop small landholdings. It states that ownership of all natural resources shall belong to the nation, which shall grant concessions to exploit those resources. This article also banned, until the 1992 reforms, the ownership of any real property by religious institutions. Foreigners were not allowed direct ownership of lands or waters within 100 kilometers of the borders or 50 kilometers along the shores. Article 123 established labor rights, including a maximum limit of eight hours of work a day, the right of workers to organize, the right to strike, and, most interestingly, the enactment of a social security law. Article 130 detailed numerous restrictions on churches, including no legal standing for religious groups; although it called for marriage as a civil contract, it stipulated that ministers be Mexican by birth, that churches obtain government permission to build new places of worship, that ministers not inherit real property, and that ministers never publicly or in privately organized groups criticize the laws of the nation or the government. These iconic articles and the principles they represent are not necessarily respected or enforced, even to this day. For example, Walmart of Mexico, which employs some 150,000 workers, gave out vouchers valid only in their own stores as part of employee salaries in 2008, in direct violation of the prohibition against companies paying salaries in anything but legal tender. More recently, in the past decade, workers at a labor camp near Guadalajara were being exploited and were prevented from leaving the farm by their employers in collaboration with local police, a common situation in rural employment before the revolution. The company was supplying Walmart and major grocery chains with produce and had received loans from the World Bank. After workers escaped from the premises and informed local authorities about conditions there, despite an investigation, heavy fines, and arrests, ultimately the responsible employers were released, the fines were not levied, and the World Bank continued to support this company. In spite of the reverence with which Mexicans hold the Constitution, today more than four out of ten believe that it does not represent real conditions in Mexico.

What was the cultural impact of the Mexican Revolution on painting, music, and literature?

The Mexican Revolution of 1910 influenced many aspects of Mexico's development, but relatively little is known of the tremendous impact it had on culture in and outside of Mexico. The social aspects of the revolutionary ideology influenced the content, methodology, and philosophy of art, music, and literature. Of these three cultural spheres, art was the most widely affected. A generation of artists, including Diego Rivera, José Clemente Orozco, and David Alfaro Siqueiros believed that painting should be a medium accessible to all

Mexicans, regardless of their social class. These artists argued that if they painted only on canvas, their art would be appreciated only by a small group of Mexicans who could afford to buy it and keep it in their homes and offices. Their view was shared by José Vasconcelos, the first minister of public education in the 1920s, who used public funding to support artists and encourage them to paint murals on the walls of government buildings, using the fresco (wet plaster) technique. These projects often involved large physical spaces and therefore incorporated the contributions of other artists and assistants, supporting another philosophical concept: that art could be a collaborative venture. But many of these artists also wanted to use their art to convey a social or political message—for example, that the Spanish exploited and abused the indigenous population during the colonization of New Spain and that the politicians and entrepreneurial class in the 1930s and 1940s were corrupt. In 1957, Siqueiros proposed to the government that artists be allowed to pay their federal taxes with their art, which the state agreed to, thus increasing the potential for more artworks to end up in a public venue. This decision was formalized legally in 1975.

In literature, Mexican novelists such as Mariano Azuela brought to life many themes of the revolution and the failures of the postrevolutionary regimes. Azuela's *The Underdogs*, for example, became the most widely read fictional work in the public school system, influencing the views of generations of Mexican adults. Other contemporary authors took up important indigenous themes, presenting the native cultures in a new, highly favorable light. The vibrancy of cultural activity in Mexico during the postrevolutionary era was viewed abroad as providing a creative and supportive environment for foreign artists, photographers, novelists, and craftspeople, including D. H. Lawrence, who spent two years in Mexico and wrote *The Plumed Serpent* about indigenous culture, and Katherine Anne Porter, who worked in Mexico from 1918 to 1921, wrote a number of stories set in Mexico, and publicized the ongoing cultural changes in a work of nonfiction, *Outline of Mexican Popular Arts and Crafts*, in 1922. The revolution also stimulated the articulation of cultural themes organic to Mexico, even in classical music, represented by *Sinfonia India*, the widely performed work of the composer Carlos Chávez, who used his leadership of Mexico's National Conservatory of Music, Mexico's Symphonic Orchestra, and the National Institute of Fine Arts to promote indigenous themes in musical compositions and performances and in other mediums. These indigenous themes have become well known outside of the country through the international performances of the Ballet Foklórico de México since 1952.

THE EVOLUTION OF MODERN POLITICAL STRUCTURES AFTER 1920

Why did the assassination of President-elect Álvaro Obregón alter Mexico's political future?

General Álvaro Obregón was president of Mexico from 1920 to 1924 and the first to complete a presidential term after the implementation of the 1917 Constitution. His administration was followed by that of Plutarco Elías Calles (1924–28), another northern revolutionary general. One of the central provisions incorporated into the Constitution in response to Porfirio Díaz's blatant abuse in maintaining himself in office for seven consecutive periods was Article 83, which prohibited a president from serving a term more than once, regardless of whether he had been elected or appointed previously. Obregón, politically ambitious and desirous of becoming president a second time, persuaded his supporters in Congress to amend the Constitution to permit nonconsecutive reelection, allowing him to run for the presidency in 1928. Many army officers, civilians, and students were strongly opposed to his running for reelection, and some were murdered by government forces in 1927. Nevertheless, Obregón won the election; but shortly thereafter, before taking office, he was assassinated by a Catholic fanatic. His unexpected death set in motion a series of crucial political changes.

Because Mexico does not have a vice president, in such a situation the Constitution provides a process whereby the Congress chooses a temporary president and then holds a new election. Anticipating the new election in 1929 and wanting to create stability in the postrevolutionary leadership, General Calles and other prominent military and civilian politicians established a national political party, the National Party of the Revolution (PNR), and ran a candidate for the presidency. Calles himself hoped to use the party to further his own ambitions, but he was unable to extend his influence beyond June 1935. This was when his former protégé, General Lázaro Cárdenas, who had won the 1934 election as the PNR's second presidential candidate, exiled his mentor to the United States. The PNR (later the Institutional Revolutionary Party, PRI) became the essential political vehicle for legitimizing presidential and government nominees for political office, winning every gubernatorial race until 1989, most Senate and district congressional seats until the 1990s, and all presidential races until 2000. Popular opinion, strongly against presidential reelection, forced the Calles faction to reamend the Constitution in 1928 to reaffirm the principle of no reelection. This has been inviolable in theory and in practice since 1929. Obregón's death set in motion two features of Mexican politics that characterized most of the twentieth century. First, presidents could become powerful, personalist decision-makers, but only for the length of their terms. Second, self-perpetuating personal leaders like Díaz would be replaced by a perpetual political organization (later named the PRI) allowing a rotating pool of ambitious politicians to govern Mexico for seven decades.

What was the influence of Plutarco Elías Calles on the formation of a modern Mexican state?

Plutarco Elías Calles was one of a generation of self-made revolutionaries who were born in the 1870s and supported the Constitutionalist Army during the revolution. From Sonora, he became involved during the initial phase of the revolution in support of Madero. Calles reached the rank of brigadier general by 1914, having joined the Constitutionalists in February 1913. He then served as the military commander and provisional governor of his home state from 1915 to 1917, and then as the constitutional governor from 1917 to 1919. He did not become a senior general during the revolution, only reaching the rank of division general in 1920. He served as a cabinet member five times and twice as secretary of war, defeating antigovernment forces during an army rebellion in 1929. The political disciple of Álvaro Obregón, Calles ran for the presidency in 1923–24, becoming president in 1924 and serving a full term.

Calles made three notable contributions to the modern Mexican state, two while in the presidency and the third after leaving office. Historians correctly attribute many of the basic public financial institutions to the Calles presidency. Calles surrounded himself with capable individuals, including Alberto J. Pani, the treasury secretary, and Manuel Gómez Morín, later the cofounder of the National Action Party (PAN). Gómez Morín was instrumental in devising important financial legislation, including that which established the Bank of Mexico, Mexico's equivalent of the US Federal Reserve Bank. The creation of the bank and other credit institutions helped stabilize the economy and encourage economic growth.

In contrast to his institutional support for economic stability, Calles, an orthodox revolutionary who initially believed in the radical articles incorporated into the Constitution of 1917, decided to impose severe restrictions on the Catholic Church. As a result, the Catholic clergy decided to boycott masses, and a popular rebellion arose among practicing Catholics in many states, known as the Cristero War (1926–29). Calles's successor, Emilio Portes Gil, negotiated a secret agreement with the Church to bring an end to the conflict, but the relationship between church and state remained strained for decades. More important, these events reinforced state superiority over the Catholic Church. The state nevertheless moderated the application of some restrictions until definitive reforms were enacted in the early 1990s, eliminating the most offensive restrictions.

Finally, Álvaro Obregón won the presidential election as Calles's successor in 1928 but was assassinated before taking office, leaving Mexico in a highly vulnerable political situation. Calles persuaded a top group of generals and civilian politicians to create a national party, the National Revolutionary Party (PNR), to provide Mexico's political leadership and maintain control over the political system, an institution that grew into the Institutional Revolutionary Party (PRI), the party that dominated the political scene for the rest of the twentieth century.

What is the National Revolutionary Party?

As the leading student of the establishment of the National Revolutionary Party (PNR), Luis Javier Garrido has noted that the party's formation was largely the brainchild of President Plutarco Elías Calles. Calles believed that a strong Mexican state could not be created or survive without a national political organization that combined all military and civilian revolutionaries under the umbrella of a central authority. Calles, leaving office after the assassination of President-elect Obregón, recognized the importance of creating such an organization to provide unity during the difficult political period that followed. He and his collaborators worked in 1928–29 to create the bylaws of the party, which brought together some 148 state and regional political organizations representing twenty-eight states and entities in Mexico. The party received financial support from the federal government, initially through monies withheld from federal bureaucrats' paychecks.

The party has undergone numerous structural changes, but the most important institutions established in the original 1929 statues, the National Executive Committee (CEN), the state committees, and the municipal committees, remain intact. The CEN became the most influential decision-making body. In reality, between 1934 and the late 1990s, the president of the CEN was designated by the incumbent president, thus providing Mexico's chief executive a direct link to the selection of candidates for national, state, and local offices, the most important of which were governors. Because the PNR was an amalgam of so many parties and political factions, its ideological composition was broad and diverse.

What ultimately became essential to the party's structure were its corporatist pillars of support, composed of the most influential political and professional groups in Mexico. In the 1930s, the leadership of the National Executive Committee included an agrarian secretary and a labor secretary. These secretaries represented the two most populous groups of supporters, led by the dominant labor unions of the day, the National Peasant Federation and the Mexican Federation of Labor. In 1938, when the PNR changed its name to the Party of the Mexican Revolution (PRM), it added a third secretary to represent the "popular" sector. This sector included numerous professional organizations and white-collar workers who were gathered under a large confederation, similar to peasants and workers, known as the National Federation of Popular Organizations. Briefly, under the influence of President Cárdenas, the party added a fourth sector, the military, but it was short-lived, and President Manuel Avila Camacho (1940–46) removed it, suggesting instead that the military could be represented in the popular sector. These multiple organizations provided a huge base of support for the party through the following decades.

Who was Lázaro Cárdenas and how did he influence Mexico's political model?

Lázaro Cárdenas was born in a small community in Michoacán in 1895. He joined the revolution as a second captain in 1913 in support of the Constitutionalists. During the ensuing decade, he fought in numerous battles, including those against the forces of Zapata and Villa, and served under his political mentor, General Plutarco Elías Calles. He also supported the government against army rebellions in 1923 and 1929, as well as against the Cristero Rebellion in 1928. He reached the rank of division general in 1928. He served as governor of his home state, president of the National Revolutionary Party (PNR), and secretary of national defense, a position from which he resigned in 1934 to run as the PNR's candidate for president.

Calles apparently believed, when he influenced the decision to make Cárdenas the PNR's first official candidate for a full presidential term, that Cárdenas would acquiesce to Calles's leadership. In other words, Calles thought that he would be the power behind the throne. Cárdenas, unwilling to be subservient to Calles, used his political skills to outmaneuver the former president, forcefully exiling him to the United States in June 1935, less than seven months after taking office. In doing so, President Cárdenas introduced a major tenet of twentieth-century Mexican politics: that presidents would exercise control over the political system during, not after, their terms. Another contribution to the Mexican political model during Cárdenas's presidency was the development of some essential features of the PNR, as well as the corporatist structure linking the state and various occupational groups. Cárdenas essentially created a formal relationship between his party and organized labor and peasant organizations, as well as most leading professional organizations. He sanctioned the inclusion of huge labor confederations in the party and therefore gave them the state's stamp of approval, establishing a symbiotic relationship that lasted for decades. He tried to do the same with the private sector, requiring firms of a certain size to join state-initiated business organizations while excluding them from the party itself. Essentially, he created official channels of communication between the state and the most influential Mexican economic and political actors.

Finally, Cárdenas altered the social and economic tone of his administration to favor, at least rhetorically and sometimes in practice, the interests of the working classes, handing out land at a dramatically increased pace and encouraging a greater number of legal strikes. On the other hand, by creating new political structures, including the corporatist links mentioned earlier, he established the basic foundation for a more powerful, centralized authoritarian state.

Why did Mexico nationalize the petroleum industry in 1939?

One of the underlying causes of the Revolution of 1910 was the degree of influence foreigners exercised in Mexico. (See question on causes of the Mexican Revolution, this chapter.) During the Porfiriato from 1884 to 1911, numerous concessions were provided to foreign investors, ranging from railroad rights of way to the exploitation of subsoil minerals, including petroleum, a resource with which Mexico was handsomely endowed. The victorious revolutionaries expressed a strong sense of nationalism that grew out of the revolutionary decade between 1910 and 1920 and was codified in the Constitution of 1917, including the assignation of all subsoil rights to the Mexican nation and the stipulation that the development and exploitation of any mineral reserves be approved by the government. Another issue that emerged during the revolutionary decade and that helps explain the nationalization of 1939 was that of workers' rights. Before the revolution, strikes were discouraged, but the postrevolutionary presidents, beginning with Álvaro Obregón (1920–24), who relied on the support of organized labor to become president, encouraged labor's growth. By the 1930s, one of the economic sectors where labor–management conflicts became intense was the petroleum industry. Through the government labor arbitration board, Lázaro Cárdenas, who became president in 1934, legalized more strikes by labor during his administration than any of his predecessors.

All of Mexico's oil was being extracted by US and European companies. A recently formed labor union, whose demands for better pay and benefits were rejected by the oil companies, took its case to the Federal Conciliation and Arbitration Board, which ruled in favor of the union and allowed it to conduct a legal strike. The board issued a ruling against the companies, requiring them to pay millions in back wages. The companies refused to comply with the decision, taking their grievances to the Mexican Supreme Court, which ruled against their appeal. President Cárdenas, responding to the intractability of the firms, most of which refused to abide by the court's decision, decided he had no alternative but to expropriate most of the companies' holdings in Mexico, creating the foundation for Petróleos Mexicanos (Pemex), Mexico's state-owned company. The government assessed the value of those holdings, which the firms also contested. The US State Department did an independent valuation of their worth and found the Mexican government's price to be generous and above the State Department's own appraisal. Before Cárdenas announced his decision on March 18, 1938, he was viewed by many groups in Mexico, including the Catholic hierarchy, the business community, religious Mexicans, and the political right, in a negative and controversial light. The day after his announcement, most Mexicans responded instantly, enthusiastically, and patriotically in support of the president's decision. Even the Catholic Church actively took up collections to help pay for the companies. As was the case elsewhere in Latin America and the Third World, the decision led to a surge in nationalistic sentiment among the Mexican population. President José López Portillo (1976–82), a college student at that time, was influenced years later in his own decision to nationalize Mexico's banks by what happened in 1938. Cárdenas's political legacy following this decision made him Mexico's most popular president for the remainder of the twentieth century.

Did Mexico participate in World War II?

The relationship between Mexico and the United States immediately before World War II was often tense. President Cárdenas's decision to nationalize the petroleum industry in March 1939 only exacerbated the difficulties. Given its historical experience with US intervention from the mid-nineteenth century, Mexico ollowed a strong noninterventionist foreign policy in the postrevolutionary decades. Mexico, therefore, rarely pursued a leadership position in Latin American regional affairs, let alone had any inclination to become involved in international conflicts. When the Japanese forces attacked Pearl Harbor and the United States declared war on the Axis powers, the US government viewed South America as a potential source of strong German influence and infiltration. Therefore, the border regions and the desolate areas of Baja California were considered to pose potential threats to the US security, one possibility being Japanese infiltration along the Pacific coast.

Unlike Brazil, which allowed the United States to use its territory as a base of operations for US Air Force flights to Africa, which provided crucial logistical support for Allied forces against the Germans in North Africa, Mexico did not ally itself with the United States. Instead, it maintained a low-key but modestly collaborative attitude toward its northern neighbor. The Secretariat of National Defense increased its focus on the northern military regions and brought former president and general Lázaro Cárdenas back on active duty to take charge of a regional military command. Mexico also accepted $39 million in lend-lease credits from the United States for improved training and weaponry. Near the end of the war, Mexico declared war on the Axis powers for attacking its oil tankers, which were transporting crude to the United States. It joined the United States by sending a small, expeditionary air force unit, the 201st Squadron, to participate in combat in the Philippines in 1945. It received a commendation from General Douglas MacArthur, commander of United States Forces in the Pacific. That squadron became highly revered in Mexico, and many of its officers achieved top posts in the Mexican Air Force. Mexico's most useful contribution to the US military effort was the provision of human resources to the United States to make up for the loss of workers in unskilled jobs, including those in railroad track maintenance and agricultural harvesting. Mexico also acceded to requests from the United States to increase the production of certain goods that were needed for the war effort and could not be imported from traditional sources, including opium-producing poppies.

When did civilian leadership take control of the Mexican political system?

One of the most admirable achievements of the Mexican political model in the twentieth century was the ability of the political leadership to maintain continuous civilian control over the military, something no other country in Latin America, with the exception of Costa Rica, accomplished. This remarkable achievement occurred incrementally after the Revolution of 1910. One way to measure the influence of military officers serving in national political office is to examine the percentage of first-time officeholders in each administration. The data suggest several patterns. The highest percentage occurred under Venustiano Carranza's 1914–20 administration, when 49 percent of the leading politicians were veteran officers. When General Obregón became president in 1920, about 40 percent of national political figures were combat veterans. The presence of the officer corps in top posts continued at an average level of 30 percent during the administrations of Presidents Calles, Portes Gil, Ortiz Rubio, and Rodríguez, from 1924 to

1934. All of these presidents, with the exception of the congressionally appointed interim president Portes Gil, were revolutionary generals.

Despite the fact that he was a general and leader of the victorious revolutionaries by 1929, General Calles, even while president, recognized the need to reduce the political role of the officer corps in Mexican politics. He reduced the number of high-ranking officers by a fourth (from 40 to 30 percent) of what it had been under his mentor and predecessor, General Obregón. He set in motion the professionalization of the officer corps, initiating a process of weeding out self-made generals with little or no formal military education. When Lázaro Cárdenas achieved the presidency in 1934 and independence from Calles in 1935, he believed the best way to keep the military under control was to make it one of the four sectors of the recently created National Revolutionary Party (PNR). While half of the state governors continued to be military officers during his administration, he dramatically reduced the proportion of career officers (excluding those in the defense and navy ministries) to only 12 percent of cabinet posts. General Manuel Avila Camacho succeeded Cárdenas in the presidency in 1940, the last officer to achieve this position, and reversed Cárdenas's strategy, eliminating the military sector from the party structure. He too allowed the same small percentage of officers to serve in his cabinet and somewhat reduced their presence as governors. Civilian supremacy, however, truly dates from 1946, when Miguel Alemán became president, the first civilian to do so since Portes Gil. He eliminated all officers from the cabinet except those in the two military ministries. He also nominated civilian governors, allowing only 13 percent of officers, compared with 40 percent during his predecessor's administration, and allowed only 5 percent of senators to have military backgrounds, the lowest figure until 1976. Although an important general competed actively for the presidency in 1952, civilian supremacy was already well entrenched.

What is the Alemán generation and what were its consequences for Mexican politics?

The "Alemán generation" refers to those politicians who collaborated with and were of the same generation as President Miguel Alemán (1946–52). They were referred to collectively as the Alemán generation because, as a group, they made numerous important contributions to the evolving Mexican political model that endured for decades. The group was characterized by its youth and civilian origins. Like the president himself, its members were ambitious politicians born largely during the first decade of the twentieth century. They are considered the first postrevolutionary generation in that they typically did not serve in combat, they came from lower-middle- and middle-class backgrounds, and they were well educated, most of them having graduated from preparatory school and college. Many were prominent student leaders, having participated in the presidential campaign against Obregón's reelection in 1927–28 and in favor of the candidacy of José Vasconcelos, a civilian who opposed the first official presidential candidate of the National Revolutionary Party (PNR) in the special election of 1929 to replace an interim president. No generation of politicians, before or since, has participated as actively in student politics as this group.

The Alemán generation was also a product of the increasing dominance of the National University of Mexico and the National Preparatory School, located in the capital, as well as the National School of Law. More than half of the president's generation graduated from the National University and nearly two-fifths from the National Preparatory School, figures that have never been equaled before or since. The excellent education of this generation dramatically enhanced the importance of national, public educational institutions in the formation and recruitment of Mexican political leaders, while the role of other political institutions, such as parties, declined. Finally, the Alemán generation, not that of Carlos Salinas, represents the first generation to have introduced a technocratic leadership. Two-thirds of Alemán's collaborators were college graduates—a figure that was not equaled until the 1964–70 administration of Gustavo Díaz Ordaz. By placing a high value on formal education, especially among assistant secretaries in cabinet-level agencies, Alemán increased the number and influence of politicians from the middle class and demonstrated that pursuing a career in the federal bureaucracy was the most important way to achieve upward political mobility during the reign of the Institutional Revolutionary Party (PRI).

What is the Institutional Revolutionary Party?

The Institutional Revolutionary Party (PRI) dominated Mexican politics from 1929 through 2000. It was the third version of the original National Revolutionary Party (PNR) founded by former president Calles and his collaborators in 1929. It was, in turn, reconstituted as the Party of the Mexican Revolution (PRM) in 1938 by President Cárdenas. On January 18, 1946, President Manuel Ávila Camacho decided to change the party's name, designating it as the Institutional Revolutionary Party. His rationale for making this name change was that it suggested to the citizenry, as well as to active PRI members, that the Mexican state, and the party that represented it, had achieved an institutionalized phase of political development after the violent decade of the revolution. It is worth noting that the name of the party evolved only one word at a time, from "national," to "Mexican," to "institutional."

These words are revealing about the attitudes of the party's leadership. In the first place, it was crucial to retain the word "revolutionary" in all three names, given that its leaders wanted to retain the image of their party as the only legitimate representative of the ideology of the revolution. They believed, and succeeded for many years, in officially identifying the PRI and its antecedents with the revolution and the state.

This attitude explains why many Mexicans referred to the PRI as the official party, as the government, and as the state. The party reinforced this perception by choosing the three colors of the Mexican flag—green, white, and red—as its own partisan colors. Not only was this visual image valuable during political campaigns, but it was critical to numerous illiterate voters who used the colors to identify PRI candidates on the ballot.

The concern of the original founders to establish a truly national political party organization explains why the word "national" was used in combination with "revolution." After a decade, the altered version of the name, the "Party of the Mexican Revolution," took on a more specific legitimizing function, suggesting again that it was the true party of the Mexican Revolution. That redesignation involved important structural changes in the organization of the party, designed to incorporate a large number of partisans from various sectors of society. When President Ávila Camacho and party leaders altered the party's name for the final time, they did so to reinforce the perception that the party's postrevolutionary achievements had become permanent and that the party would provide stability and continuity into the future. President Carlos Salinas de Gortari (1988–94) considered changing the party's name again, but ultimately was persuaded to leave it untouched.

From 1946 through 1987, the party essentially functioned as a vehicle for maintaining itself in power, having monopolized most elective and appointive positions since the 1930s. From 1988 forward, it faced increasing electoral competition at all levels and went through numerous adjustments to transform itself into a competitive political party. Despite its major losses in the presidential elections of 2000 and 2006, it won the presidency in 2012. It continues to boast the largest and broadest partisan base, making it a political force to reckon with in the future.

What is the Mexican economic miracle?

The "Mexican economic miracle" refers to the decades during which Mexico experienced its longest period of sustained economic growth. Most observers date the so-called miracle from the late 1940s to the early 1970s, concentrated in four presidential administrations: those of Miguel Alemán (1946–52), Adolfo Ruiz Cortines (1952–58), Adolfo López Mateos (1958–64), and Gustavo Díaz Ordaz (1964–70). Economic growth during these years averaged a consistent 3–4 percent yearly and was characterized by low inflation rates. By the 1960s, gross domestic product was averaging 7 percent. Most economists attribute this growth to several important conditions. Most commonly, they point to the import substitution strategy pursued by the Mexican government, which protected domestic industry by means of high tariffs on consumer goods and allowed the importation of capital goods. The administration of Miguel Alemán introduced and emphasized this industrialization strategy. Alemán and his successors expanded public investment in infrastructure and transportation, and Mexico began rapidly to shift from a rural to an urban society. It witnessed a huge internal shift in the population from small villages and towns to urban centers, as the percentage of Mexicans employed in agriculture declined and those in manufacturing and services increased significantly. Moreover, in the two decades preceding this period of growth, Mexico dramatically increased the number of children enrolled in school, thus reducing illiteracy and enhancing the educational preparation of the workforce.

While this period has been traditionally viewed in positive terms because of the long-term growth of Mexico's gross domestic product, detailed studies by economists demonstrate that, contrary to popular perceptions, even though Mexico increased the size of its economy and its productivity, most of the economic benefits were not shared by the majority of the economically active population. As late as 1994, more than half of Mexico's population was classified by the World Bank as living in poverty (i.e., earning less than $2 per capita daily), and half of that population was classified as living in absolute poverty (earning less than $1 per capita daily). The contradictions between general economic growth, the inequality in the distribution of that growth, and per capita growth is reflected in the fact that Mexico was ranked in 2016 as the fifteenth-largest economy in the world but a mere seventy-two in per capita gross domestic product.

What is the National Action Party?

The National Action Party (PAN) is currently a leading political party that was founded in 1939 by dissident politicians in the Mexican government and other leading political activists searching for an ideological alternative to the National Revolutionary Party (PNR), founded by former president Calles and his collaborators in 1929. A notable founder of the PAN was Manuel Gómez Morín, a financial and political supporter of José Vasconcelos's opposition presidential campaign in 1929 and an influential contributor to Mexico's public financial institutions in the 1920s. The PAN was founded at the highpoint of Lázaro Cárdenas's administration. Many of its founders were opposed to policies implemented by Cárdenas and the direction of postrevolutionary governments. In particular they were critical of the government's orientation toward the incorporation of socialist principles in public education, the anti-Catholic rhetoric of numerous government party officials, and, most significantly, the virtual political monopoly exercised by the Party of the Mexican Revolution (PRM, the PNR's successor in 1938) over every elected office from mayor to president.

The PAN was Mexico's oldest opposition party until it won the presidential election in 2000. It grew very slowly under politically adverse circumstances at the state and local levels for decades. Its politicians and supporters were constantly harassed and, worse, sometimes killed during the 1940s, 1950s, and 1960s. It did not make significant headway against the

Institutional Revolutionary Party (PRI) (which replaced the PRM in 1946) until the electoral reforms of 1964, which assigned a small number of "party seats" to the opposition parties in the Chamber of Deputies, Mexico's lower house. These positions, combined with a small number of congressional districts the PAN actually was able to win, allowed it to have a voice in the legislative branch and to reward its party faithful with elected political offices. In the mid-1960s, its congressional candidates obtained 12 percent of the vote. By 2000, they earned more than 30 percent.

The PAN, in an attempt to achieve stronger ideological coherence, has kept its active party membership small, thus limiting its partisan base in an era of highly competitive elections since 1994. It has developed its electoral strength regionally rather than nationally and produced its greatest successes in urban centers in those areas. It lost ground in the 1988 presidential election, when Cuauhtémoc Cárdenas obtained the second-highest number of votes for president, but it made a comeback in 1994, winning a quarter of the votes for the presidency. More important, during the 1990s, it used its regional strengths and its pro-democratic ideology to increase its appeal at the state and local levels. By 1997, the PAN, the Party of the Democratic Revolution and smaller opposition parties represented 50 percent of the population at the state and local levels, that figure increasing to 61 percent in 2001. The PAN won the presidency in 2000 and 2006, controlling the executive branch until 2012.

THE DECLINE OF THE INSTITUTIONAL REVOLUTIONARY PARTY AND THE MEXICAN MODEL

What was the Tlatelolco Student Massacre of 1968 and what were its long-term political consequences?

On October 2, 1968, in the wake of student protests at the National Autonomous University of Mexico (UNAM) and other public institutions (against the occupation of a vocational high school by police and also of UNAM by the army, violating the principle of university autonomy), thousands of students gathered at the Plaza of the Three Cultures in the Tlatelolco neighborhood of Mexico City for a peaceful demonstration against the government. The army was sent in to maintain order. Shots were fired from nearby apartment buildings, setting off a violent response from the troops. Hundreds of students and bystanders were killed and wounded by the army, and in the aftermath hundreds of students, intellectuals, and professors were imprisoned by the government. Many years later it was revealed that President Gustavo Díaz Ordaz purposely provoked the violent response by sending snipers dressed in civilian clothes from his own presidential guard battalion to fire on army troops. Many analysts believe he pursued such a repressive strategy in part because the government had invested millions of dollars to sponsor the Olympic Games, scheduled to begin just ten days after the protest.

It is generally agreed that the events of 1968 were the most important catalyst of a crisis of legitimacy for the Mexican government and the political model that had long been pursued by the incumbent Institutional Revolutionary Party (PRI). Not only did the government repression shock Mexicans from all social classes, it also tarnished its image abroad, especially in the United States. Most important, it set in motion numerous political forces that ultimately contributed to a democratic transition in the 1980s and 1990s and to the subsequent defeat of the PRI in the presidential election of 2000.

The short- to medium-term consequence of the student massacre was the radicalization of a generation of students who became political activists. Some of these individuals joined small leftist organizations. A number of these organizations eventually contributed to the expansion of the electoral Left, serving as a partial basis of support for Cuauhtémoc Cárdenas's presidential campaign in 1988, and the establishment of the Party of the Democratic Revolution in 1989. Other individuals joined peasant groups in protests against the government, and some became involved with indigenous groups, including what became the Zapatista Army of National Liberation (EZLN) in Chiapas in 1994. Many Mexican intellectuals reacted strongly to the repression, encouraging some people to become more critical and independent of the state, and others to join or form opposition parties. Finally, in broad terms, the student repression encouraged the growth of civic organizations from all sectors of society, representing business people, women, priests and nuns who were advocates of liberation theology, intellectuals, and others.

What was the "Dirty War" in Mexico?

Throughout South America during the 1970s and 1980s, the military and its conservative civilian allies were engaged in a violent conflict against leftist political groups for control of their respective political systems. Many individuals involved in this struggle viewed the leftist opposition as a threat to their country's civilization and survival. With the help of the armed forces, these groups set in motion repressive, authoritarian regimes that committed horrific human rights abuses, during which many people disappeared from their homes or off the street. Thus, scholars referred to these events as a "dirty war" and the victims as "the disappeared." Mexico experienced its own "Dirty War," but it was never as deeply or widely entrenched as elsewhere in the region, nor did it involve a takeover of the political apparatus by the armed forces, either directly or indirectly. The persecution of left-wing political activists, or individuals often only remotely linked to such activists through friendship or family, began in earnest after the 1968 student movement.

After imprisoning many activists following the tragic massacre of students and bystanders in October 1968, the government instructed its security forces to persecute other potential leaders. In December 1970, President Luis Echeverría, the former minister of government who oversaw the massacre of student demonstrators under his predecessor, took office and began his own contradictory strategy of dealing with dissident groups. He recruited some former student leaders to the government and pursued others through the Federal Security Agency in the Secretariat of Government or directly through the armed forces. A number of groups resisted the violent reprisals, and several guerrilla organizations came into existence during the Echeverría administration (1970–76).

The most notable guerrilla movement in opposition to government policies during this era was that of Lucio Cabañas, a former rural schoolteacher from a peasant family. Cabañas was a leader of the National Federation of Peasant Societies, a group independent of the government, and he eventually organized a guerrilla movement in the poor southern state of Guerrero. The movement operated from 1968 until 1974, when Cabañas was killed under mysterious circumstances by army forces. During this period, units of the Mexican Army were involved in human rights abuses throughout Mexico, including the murder of prisoners. Troops killed prisoners by tossing them out of airplanes and more commonly by executing them at military bases, notably at Military Base No. 1 in Mexico City. Only two general officers were ever tried for such abuses after the National Action Party (PAN) came to power in 2000, and although genocide charges were brought against former president Echeverría, he was never convicted.

What was the impact of the 1964 electoral reforms?

In the second half of the twentieth century, the Institutional Revolutionary Party (PRI), facing increasing criticism of its semiauthoritarian political model, decided to introduce electoral reforms that altered the distribution of majority districts and added what became known as party deputies to the federal legislative branch. Prior to the reforms, the lower house of

Congress, the Chamber of Deputies, consisted of 178 congressional districts. Between 1949 and 1961, the PRI lost only 33 (4 percent!) of a total of 807 district seats. In 1964, it decided to alter the composition of the congressional seats, introducing an additional 36–41 party deputy seats during the congressional sessions from 1964 to 1979. The law relied on a formula based on the percentage of votes cast for congressional candidates in each election. The PRI's underlying rationale for introducing this change was to create the impression that the electoral system was more democratic and competitive than was actually the case, assigning these seats only to opposition party candidates. For example, in the 1964 elections, in addition to the 178 seats assigned to the victorious candidate in each congressional district, the PRI having won 175 districts (fairly or through fraud), 36 additional seats were assigned to three other parties. The majority of those seats were allocated to the National Action Party (PAN) up to 1979. In 1977, President José López Portillo passed new legislation that not only increased the number of majority districts to 300 seats, but also created a plurinominal system to replace the party deputy system, allocating to the new system 100 additional seats, a fourth of all congressional seats. Years later, an additional 100 plurinominal seats were added, bringing the total to 500 seats, the current number in the Chamber of Deputies. In early 2017, the PRI proposed reducing the plurinominal seats to 100, thereby having only 400 seats in the Chamber of Deputies.

The 1964 reforms establishing the party deputy system (which ultimately became the plurinominal system) had a significant, long-term impact on the composition of the legislative branch and the composition of party leadership in the opposition parties, particularly on the PAN, which was the first opposition party to defeat the PRI for the presidency in 2000. Because the PAN could not elect many of its most active and notable partisan supporters to the majority districts, the party leaders designated candidates who would receive the party or plurinominal seats. This process centralized control over nominations in the hands of the party bureaucracy in Mexico City, thus inhibiting more rapid development of regional and municipal party affiliates that could promote successful candidates to the only national offices PAN politicians could win: seats in the legislative branch. Those legal changes helped institutionalize the importance of PAN leadership and the national party bureaucracy from the Federal District.

What were the leading political characteristics of Mexico's semiauthoritarian model?

Some features of Mexico's unique and often successful political model that evolved from the 1930s through the 1980s explain, in part, its longevity. The most important of these were a self-perpetuating political elite that represented succeeding generations of younger politicians; a civilian leadership that institutionalized its supremacy and control over the military and the revolutionary veterans; a pragmatic ideology that leaders legitimized in the rhetoric of the 1910 revolution; the establishment of a corporatist system that linked the most populous occupational groups to the federal government and the party; a strong national party that served as an electoral vehicle; and the legitimacy of the presidency, reinforced by the principle of "no reelection," consecutive or otherwise.

The leadership of the Institutional Revolutionary Party (PRI) and its antecedent parties and the federal government developed a process by which they were able to satisfy a broad group of ambitious politicians who represented a wide range of ideologies, rewarding them with government posts in all three branches of government and in all levels, local, state, and national. The president was at the apex of this system and exercised the greatest influence over nominees for elective office and appointees for top posts in the judicial and executive branches. With the advent of the generation of President Miguel Alemán (1946–52), a postrevolutionary group of civilian lawyers took control of the national and state political

system, and dramatically reduced the influence of combat veterans and professional military officers on the political system,
establishing a firm foundation for civilian control from 1946
to the present. Government and party leaders were more
pragmatic than ideological, creating a broad ideological umbrella under which they could invite talented and ambitious
politicians to join forces with their collaborators. The leadership, beginning with President Lázaro Cárdenas, encouraged
labor and peasant organizations to develop formal ties with
the party and the government, cementing a relationship that
continues to some extent today with the PRI. It also created
nonvoluntary business organizations that channeled private
sector demands to appropriate federal agencies. It developed
an effective grassroots electoral organization whose primary
goal was to keep the PRI and its supporters in power rather
than to take power away from other political organizations.
Finally, it assigned significant informal powers to the presidency, further legitimating its control and influence over the
entire political model and creating an expectation, which still
exists in part, that the president should exercise power firmly
and definitively.

What were the consequences of the nationalization of the banks in 1982?

During the presidency of Luis Echeverría, the Mexican government began acquiring an increasing number of businesses,
ranging from fertilizer companies to restaurants. From 1972
through the end of the decade, state ownership of private firms
tripled. At the end of his administration, Echeverría took over
agricultural properties in northwestern Mexico, alienating the
private sector. When his successor, José López Portillo, took
office in 1976, he made an effort to reestablish positive relations with the private sector. During the early part of his administration, he was successful in achieving that goal. But as
Mexico's economic situation became more difficult later in his

term, provoked by the dramatic decline in oil prices, on which the government under both administrations had become increasingly dependent, wealthy Mexicans began taking their funds out of the country and depositing or investing them in the United States. After consulting only with two of his collaborators, López Portillo surprised the Mexican public, fellow politicians, and the private sector with his decision to nationalize all the banks. Unlike the petroleum industry, the banks were Mexican-owned. The president publicly blamed the bankers for not preventing capital from being drained from the country. This decision reversed all of the president's prior efforts to strengthen the relationship between the government and the private sector. Interestingly, however, a poll taken shortly after the nationalization revealed that most small and medium-sized businesses outside the banking sector reacted favorably to the government's takeover of the banks, a reaction explained by the fact that most large banks belonged to large holding companies representing other economic sectors and that they typically gave preference to firms owned by their own holding company when making loans. It has been estimated that indirectly, through mortgages controlled by the banks, the government controlled 80–85 percent of the economy.

In the long term, this decision damaged the relationship between the private sector and the government. It was substantially repaired, however, by President Miguel de la Madrid (1982–88), who at the end of his administration returned some of the insurance companies acquired through the nationalization to the private sector. Still, some members of the private sector and several of the leading business organizations became much more politically active in opposing the government and its economic policies, setting the stage in the 1990s for businessmen to become involved in electoral politics, typically in support of the National Action Party (PAN). De la Madrid chose Carlos Salinas de Gortari as his successor, and as part of his neoliberal economic strategy, Salinas sold off all of the banks to prominent capitalists. In the long run, however, ownership of these banks shifted to foreign companies, which presently control more than 90 percent of banking firms in Mexico.

Did Mexico's economic woes in the 1980s have significant political consequences?

Mexico's long-term reliance on an import substitution strategy, heavy spending of revenues from the income of the state-owned petroleum companies, and excessive borrowing of monies from US and European banks led to a major economic crisis in the last few months of the López Portillo administration (1976–82), shortly before the inauguration of President Miguel de la Madrid in December 1982. Mexico was forced to suspend payments on its foreign debt, and the new president decided to adopt severe austerity measures. Gross domestic product (adjusted for inflation) had increased an average of 8.4 percent yearly from 1977 to 1981, but collapsed to an incredible 0.1 percent during the entirety of the de la Madrid administration, from 1982 to 1988—which witnessed rates of inflation averaging 88 percent during the same time period. The government's austerity measures, including economic pacts with organized labor and the private sector, limited social spending, severely restricted wage increases, and increased prices for basic commodities, producing a drop in real wages of nearly 50 percent from 1982 to 1988.

There was talk in the Mexican media during 1983–84 of the increased potential for social violence given the breadth and depth of the impact of the economic crisis on the average Mexican's standard of living. The economic crisis and the government's policy solutions contributed to three significant, longer-term consequences. First, it further delegitimized the Mexican political model, which had relied heavily on long periods of economic growth in the early administrations to retain control. It also encouraged an increase in independent labor organizations and a decline in organized labor as a percentage of the overall economically active population. Second, combined with the federal government's inept reaction to a devastating earthquake in Mexico City in 1985, the austerity program encouraged hundreds of nongovernmental organizations to emerge, leading to a dramatic growth in civic organizations, which presented growing demands to the government. This development also encouraged the direct involvement of women in social movements, laying the groundwork for political opposition to the system and a gradual democratic transition. Third, the government leadership, in response to the severity of the crisis, decided to pursue a neoliberal economic policy solution based upon a trade-led economic strategy and a trading bloc with the United States and Canada (NAFTA), a strategy that continues to be pursued by the current administration. (See the interview with Jaime Serra Puche, Secretary of Commerce from 1982–1988, at latinamericanhistory.oxfordre.com/page/videos/.)

9

MEXICO'S DEMOCRATIC TRANSITION

How did Carlos Salinas alter the Mexican political model?

Carlos Salinas de Gortari became president of Mexico in 1988, after a highly contentious and fraudulent election. His predecessor, Miguel de la Madrid, selected his former secretary of programming and budgeting as his successor in order to keep his own internationally oriented, neoliberal economic strategy in place. Salinas surrounded himself with political technocrats, many of whom, like the president, had undergraduate degrees in economics boasted a graduate education abroad, typically at Ivy League schools in the United States, but few of whom had any experience in electoral politics. Salinas also appointed an increasing number of graduates from private universities in the capital, especially the Autonomous Technological Institute of Mexico (ITAM), to top political posts.

Salinas, in pursuing his predecessor's economic strategy, made significant changes in the political landscape, which inadvertently created a positive setting for a democratic transition from the one-party dominance of the Institutional Revolutionary Party (PRI). Among the changes he made, four stand out for their impact on the historic semiauthoritarian model. First and most strongly linked to his economic philosophy, he sought to integrate Mexico into a new economic bloc to increase its competitiveness in the global economy, proposing a North American free trade agreement with the United States, its largest trading partner, and Canada. The NAFTA treaty, which went into effect during his last year in office, moved Mexico away, for the first time, from an isolationist stance in the region to coming under the influence of multiple foreign countries. For example, it received increased attention from various US institutions and constituencies. Ultimately, this foreign influence encouraged democratization within Mexico. Second, on his own initiative, and in part to, in effect, bring Mexico into the end of the twentieth century in terms of its international human rights agreements (which contradicted constitutional restrictions on clergy in Mexico), he eliminated a number of provisions regarding relations between church and state, even though he faced opposition by many members of his own party. The elimination of these long-time restrictions encouraged activist bishops and clergy to publicly support civic organizations and electoral democracy through numerous diocesan missives. Third, in order to cultivate support from Wall Street and the US Senate, Salinas intervened in the outcome of some important state elections, including races for governor, permitting an opposition party candidate to win a governorship for the first time since 1929, sixty years after the party was founded. These state and local victories encouraged the growth of both the National Action Party (PAN) and the Party of the Democratic Revolution (PRD). Fourth, Salinas's excessive reliance on bureaucratic technocrats from the PRI, rather than on politicians with roots in elective offices and party organizations, produced a reaction within the PRI. The party changed its internal rules to require that its presidential candidate have electoral and party experience, ushering in a generation of politicians with such credentials and preparing the PRI in the long run for participation in a competitive electoral setting.

*Why is the presidential election of 1988 a benchmark
for democracy in Mexico?*

To many analysts and students of Mexican politics, 1988
will remain a significant starting point in Mexico's transition to electoral democracy. That year is significant for the
Institutional Revolutionary Party (PRI) itself because it was the
first presidential election year since 1952 in which a prominent
individual active in the party became the major opposition
party candidate. By 1986, leading politicians within the PRI
who harbored the ambition to become their party's presidential candidate realized that President Miguel de la Madrid was
going to pursue a neoliberal economic strategy that was opposed by the traditional wing of the party. This wing included
Cuauhtémoc Cárdenas, the former governor of Michoacán and
son of Mexico's most popular president, Lázaro Cárdenas, and
Porfirio Muñoz Ledo, a former president of the PRI. These two
figures, along with other leading members of the party, formed
a "Democratic Current" within the party and ultimately were
forced out of the PRI, taking a number of prominent politicians
with them. When Carlos Salinas de Gortari was designated the
PRI candidate, a number of smaller leftist parties obtained
recognition and ran against him, as did the National Action
Party (PAN), the most successful opposition party until 1988.
Although Cárdenas formed his own party, the Cardenista
Front for National Reconstruction, to support his candidacy, he
was eventually listed on the ballot under four different parties.

Salinas was not a popular choice among many PRI faith-
fuls, thus giving Cárdenas a more viable opportunity as an
opposition candidate. He campaigned vigorously, having
widespread name recognition because of his father's reputation. When the election was held, the PRI resorted to outright
fraud to alter the vote totals for the three leading candidates
after discovering that Salinas would not obtain even a simple
majority of votes. Some observers believe that Cárdenas won
the election, and on July 12, 1988, the last day his campaign,

staff members received official information (from approximately half of the balloting stations, accounting for 54.09 percent of the vote) that Cárdenas was ahead with 39.5 percent to PRI's 35.8 percent, followed by the PAN with 21.4 percent. What is most important about the results, however, is that for the first time since the 1930s, Mexican voters could understand that it actually might be possible to defeat the PRI. In short, the 1988 election became a victory for all opposition parties, strengthening increased political opposition at the state and local levels. One year later, the PAN won the first gubernatorial race since the PRI came to power. The 1988 election also led to the formation of a third significant party in Mexican politics, the Party of the Democratic Revolution (PRD), which nearly won the presidency in the 2006 elections and again came in second place in 2012. Through the PRD, the 1988 election strengthened the Mexican Left, and in spite of continuous divisions within the PRD, increased the Left's unity in the electoral arena. (For Cuauhtémoc Cárdenas's own views, see an interview at: latinamericanhistory.oxfordre.com/page/videos.)

Who is Cuauhtémoc Cárdenas and what is the Party of the Democratic Revolution?

Cuauhtémoc Cárdenas Solórzano is a Mexican politician who comes from an influential political family, beginning with his father, General Lázaro Cárdenas, president of Mexico from 1934 to 1940. To many Mexicans, his father stood out as a defender of Mexican sovereignty, having nationalized foreign oil companies in 1939. He also symbolized agrarian reform, having distributed more land to peasants than any previous president. Cuauhtémoc began his political career as a student supporter of General Miguel Henríquez Guzmán's presidential campaign in 1951 and helped support his father's leadership of the National Liberation Movement in the 1960s. He was elected senator from his home state of Michoacán before becoming governor, following in the footsteps of his father and uncle. After leaving office, he joined other prominent politicians of the Institutional Revolutionary Party (PRI) in founding the Democratic Current in 1986, a faction within the party that supported the anti-neoliberal economic strategy being pursued by President de la Madrid as well as increased political pluralism. When Carlos Salinas de Gortari was selected as the PRI's candidate, it became clear that the neoliberal policies would be continued. Cárdenas and other leading members of the Democratic Current left the PRI and formed their own small party, and Cárdenas became the party's presidential candidate in 1988. Eventually he was supported by four small parties. In the hard-fought campaign that ensued, Cárdenas officially won 37 percent of the vote to Salinas's 51 percent, and the National Action Party (PAN) candidate obtained 17 percent in an election marred by extensive fraud (see preceding entry in this chapter).

Most observers believe that Cárdenas won a larger percentage of the vote, and some believe he may have defeated Salinas. Nevertheless, even though Cárdenas lost, his electoral success gave birth in 1989 to a new, influential opposition party, the Party of the Democratic Revolution (PRD). Cárdenas presided over the party from 1989 to 1993, when he became the party's candidate a second time in the 1994 election, losing to the PRI candidate, Ernesto Zedillo. The PRD was an amalgam of left-of-center parties and numerous defectors from the PRI who favored increased pluralization, fair elections, and a return to a state-supported system of increased social expenditures. Cárdenas's success also increased opposition party representation in Congress. The establishment of the PRD encouraged alliances between it and the PAN on the state level, leading to successful gubernatorial campaigns, which continue to the present. The strength of the PRD and PAN in Congress forced significant changes in the electoral process instituted in 1996, contributing to an independent institution, the Federal Electoral Institute (renamed the National Electoral Institute), exercising complete control over the elections and providing public funding for all parties. In 1997, Cárdenas won a decisive victory as the first elected governor of the Federal District. Although he was unsuccessful in his bid to become president for the third time, in 2000, placing a distant third behind the PAN and PRI candidates, the party recovered its strength through the leadership of Andrés Manuel López Obrador, who presided over the PRD and the Mexico City government before narrowly losing to Felipe Calderón in the 2006 presidential race and Enrique Peña Nieto in 2012. After legally appealing the outcome of the election in 2012, as he had done in 2006, he broke away from the PRD and formed his own party, Morena (National Regeneration Movement), significantly reducing support for the Left, and specifically the PRD, with 11 percent compared with 8 percent for Morena in the 2015 congressional elections. PRI captured 29 percent of the votes, followed by PAN with 21 percent. (See Cuauhtémoc Cárdenas's interview at latinamericanhistory.oxfordre.com/page/videos.)

What is NAFTA and how did Carlos Salinas change Mexico's economic model?

When Carlos Salinas de Gortari became president of Mexico in 1988, he did not have a clear electoral mandate, having won the election through extensive fraud. In order to establish a greater level of legitimacy and support, he pursued a number of decisive political actions in the first six months of his administration. But his most significant, long-term strategy, which was innovative and controversial, was to stimulate Mexico's economic growth by expanding its global economic ties through the establishment of an economic trade bloc. It became apparent to economists and political leaders worldwide that most countries needed to associate themselves with other countries in order to compete globally. Salinas, who believed strongly in this concept, initially approached the European Economic Union. But the European Economic Union was overwhelmed by the task of integrating countries that were part of the former

Soviet Union and turned him down. As a result, he decided to propose to the United States and Canada the formation of a North American free trade agreement, which would reduce tariffs on the importation of hundreds of goods among the three countries. It was a controversial proposal within both Mexico and the United States. Indeed, it became an issue in the 1992 US presidential campaign, during which the independent candidate, Ross Perot, strongly criticized the concept. But Salinas, relying on a close working relationship with President George H. Bush, effectively lobbied Congress and Wall Street, stifling opposition to the proposal within his own party and censoring independent criticism. He eventually succeeded in achieving an agreement that formally went into effect January 1, 1994.

In addition to implementing NAFTA, he complemented his global economic strategy with a reversal of government ownership of many enterprises and the banks, which had been nationalized by President José López Portillo in 1982. His administration sold off numerous companies and banks, many to favored individuals, restoring control to the private sector and reestablishing better relations between the private sector and the government. This domestic and international economic strategy produced increased capital investment in Mexico from abroad and dramatically increased Mexican exports to its preferred trading partners. At the same time, however, thousands of Mexicans lost their jobs, as cheaper imports from the United States put small entrepreneurs out of business. Whereas in the United States funds were allocated to retrain US workers who also became unemployed as a result of the treaty, Mexicans had to fend for themselves. Rural farmers were hardest hit by these and other reforms, and even though the government initiated an agricultural support program known as PROCAMPO, in reality it benefited larger farms of more than 5 hectares, while those with fewer than 5 hectares accounted for only 8 percent of the program's benefits.

Finally, Salinas introduced an entirely new concept of federal assistance to local communities, through an agency called

Pronasol. Essentially, Pronasol became a distributive entity through which federal revenues were directly distributed to local communities for projects requested by those communities. The president traveled on hundreds of work trips to small municipalities during his administration to personally meet local leaders and allocate these funds. Although critics charged that the funds were used to generate legitimacy for the Institutional Revolutionary Party (PRI) government, more than half of the funds went directly to local communities. This strategy revived the importance of municipalities and served as an underlying basis for more specific antipoverty programs undertaken by Presidents Zedillo and Fox. (See the interview with Jaime Serra Puche, a major figure in the NAFTA negotiations, at latinamericanhistory.oxfordre.com/page/videos/.)

Who are the technocrats?

Generally speaking, the term "technocrats" refers to individuals, typically professional people, with specialized skills and advanced education. In Latin America, primarily in the Southern Cone, the word refers to economists who pursued a macroeconomic policy strategy in line with the conservative economic views propounded at the University of Chicago. In Mexico, the term "technocrats" takes on a different and somewhat unique meaning. Most analysts view technocrats as Mexican politicians of a special type who emerged in top leadership positions in the federal executive branch beginning in the early 1980s. The first Mexican president who can be viewed as a technocrat is Miguel de la Madrid, a graduate of the National School of Law, who completed an MA degree in public administration at Harvard University. De la Madrid was responsible for encouraging a new group of politicians to hold cabinet posts and important offices in the subcabinet, especially in economically oriented agencies ranging from trade to agriculture to the treasury. Among his most prominent appointees were Carlos Salinas de Gortari, his budget and programming secretary, and Jesús Silva Herzog, his initial treasury secretary. Both men were graduates of the National School of Economics; both obtained advanced degrees in the United States at Harvard and Yale, respectively; both pursued political careers in the federal bureaucracy; and neither man had ever held elective office.

De la Madrid, Carlos Salinas, and Ernesto Zedillo (the last three Institutional Revolutionary Party [PRI] presidents before 2000) embodied all the characteristics of technocrats just described. All three men served in the Programming and Budgeting cabinet post (which was combined with the Treasury under Salinas), making it the most strategic post for a Mexican politician with presidential ambitions. The technocrats, having trained in the United States, returned to Mexico with the belief that neoliberal economic strategies, similar to those pursued in the United States, were the long-term solution to Mexico's economic and social problems. The influence of these individuals, who shared similar career characteristics and beliefs about Mexico development policies, reached its apex under Ernesto Zedillo (1994–2000). As a faction within the PRI, they were opposed by those politicians who held different economic views and who typically were trained in more traditional disciplines and had pursued careers in the electoral arena and the party bureaucracy. Although de la Madrid has been identified as the first technocratic president, a careful examination of presidential administrations reveals that Miguel Alemán and his generation are the historical antecedents of many similar qualities, anticipating the economist technocrat by nearly forty years. Also, it is apparent that a new generation of technocrats, born in the 1960s but with somewhat different qualities, emerged in the Calderón administration. That newest generation of technocrats served in Peña Nieto's administration (2012–). Indeed, two notable examples are Luis Videgaray Caso, born in 1968, with a PhD from MIT, who became Peña Nieto's secretary of the treasury, and José Antonio Meade, born in 1969, with a PhD from Yale, who became his first secretary of foreign affairs, after serving as Calderón's treasury secretary.

When did an opposition party win its first governorship in Mexico?

The answer to this question must be qualified because it is likely that on several occasions opposition candidates won gubernatorial elections in their respective states but were not recognized as victors because of fraud perpetrated by the Institutional Revolutionary Party (PRI) at the ballot box. The most notable historical example of this occurred in San Luis Potosi as early as 1961, when Salvador Nava Martínez, a popular, politically active physician, ran against the PRI candidate for governor after being rejected by the PRI as a nominee. He ran as the candidate of the Potosino Civic Front, but was declared the loser in an election marred by widespread fraud. He was later arrested and imprisoned for political reasons in the 1960s. Three decades later, in 1991, he ran again as a gubernatorial candidate representing an alliance of opposition parties, including the National Action Party (PAN), after having won the mayoralty election in the state capital of San Luis Potosí in 1982. Again, the PRI committed widespread fraud in the election. After the PRI governor had held office for less than two weeks, following a protest march organized by Nava, President Salinas forced the governor to resign, but replaced him with another PRI politician instead of Nava.

The first opposition governor to win a gubernatorial election recognized by the government was Ernesto Ruffo Appel, who took office in Baja California on November 1, 1989, setting in motion a wave of opposition victories by the PAN, and to a lesser extent the Party of the Democratic Revolution (PRD), on the state level. Ruffo's victory was critical in convincing voters that gubernatorial candidates from other parties could indeed win an election and therefore deserved their serious consideration and votes as potential candidates. Ruffo, typical of a new generation of PAN politicians, came from a business background, had served as mayor of Ensenada from 1986 to 1988, and led local business organizations. He later served in President Fox's cabinet.

What was the Zapatista uprising of 1994 and what were its political consequences?

On January 1, 1994, a small guerrilla band of indigenous Mexicans in the poor southern state of Chiapas attacked several army posts in what became known as the Zapatista uprising. The North American Free Trade Agreement (NAFTA) with the United States and Canada formally went into effect on that date, and the Zapatistas used it as a symbol of opposition to the neoliberal economic policies of the Salinas administration. The brief and militarily ineffective uprising was put down violently by the Mexican armed forces, which committed human rights abuses in defeating the poorly armed guerrillas. Formally known as the Zapatista Army of National Liberation (EZLN), the peasants who made up the guerrillas and their active supporters had a long list of complaints against local, state, and federal authorities. They advocated agrarian reforms and opposed Salinas's revisions of the agrarian provisions in Article 27 of the Constitution. They also believed they had been effectively excluded from the political process, and they viewed their economic situation as continuing to deteriorate compared with that of most other Mexicans.

Militarily, the Zapatistas proved to be unsuccessful. Politically, however, most Mexicans were favorably predisposed to their goals, although they were opposed to their initial use of violence. The Zapatistas used the Internet effectively, both in Mexico and in the United States, to gain support, and they were equally effective in finding allies in the domestic and international media. They exercised a long-term political impact in two ways. First, they served as a catalyst for the establishment and activity of dozens of nongovernmental organizations that pressed their own social and economic demands on the government. These groups, along with the EZLN, which transformed itself into a vociferous political organization, contributed to the growth of civic organizations and to widespread support for the democratic transition of the Mexican political system. Second, although the Zapatistas never formally achieved an agreement with the Mexican government, and they have exercised little influence on the political arena in recent years, they did initiate a broader movement, found elsewhere in the region, advocating indigenous rights and municipal autonomy in Mexico. These goals have been most widely implemented in the southern state of Oaxaca.

What were the consequences of the Zapatistas for civil–military relations?

The attack by the Zapatista Army of National Liberation (EZLN) on several army installations on the morning of January 1, 1994, in part to symbolize the EZLN's objection to the North American Free Trade Agreement and what it implied for Mexican peasants, had numerous consequences for the Mexican armed forces, for the relationship between civil and military authorities, and for the military's role in determining national security policy. The uprising caught the Mexican public and the international community completely by surprise (see the immediately preceding question). As was the case some twenty-five years earlier, in 1968, when troops surrounded the student demonstrators in Tlatelolco Plaza, the army was asked to react to a difficult political problem created by civilian leaders' incompetence. The events of January 1994, however, were even more consequential for the civil–military relationship because military intelligence for more than a year before these events had warned civilian agencies of the disenchantment of these groups and the likelihood that they would take future actions against local authorities.

The armed forces' immediate suppression of the small guerrilla bands was brutal and involved widely reported human rights violations, presenting the military in a negative light in the domestic and international media. Officers in the armed forces became disgruntled with civilian security leadership and decision-making, ultimately pressuring national leaders to include the Secretariats of National Defense and Navy in the decision-making process, thus giving the military a voice in those policies it would be asked to enforce or implement. As a consequence, these officers became an effective voice in the national security subcabinet. Equally important, military dissatisfaction with its role in controlling the Zapatistas led to a unique, highly critical self-appraisal within the military in a 1995 internal memorandum that was leaked to the Mexican media. This report identified numerous institutional weaknesses and outlined concrete strategies for improvement. Many could be traced to the military's role in suppressing the Zapatista uprising. For example, the report recommended a complete overhaul of the military's electronic capabilities, which would include advanced training in computer technology and the acquisition of superior computer equipment. This recommendation, in part, was a response to the Zapatistas' successful use of the Internet in presenting their case to the public and to the international media and scholarly community. The report also recommended that the armed forces improve their intelligence-gathering efforts and establish links with counterpart civilian agencies, such as the attorney general of Mexico. Finally, the report recommended the expansion of mobile units that could be flown into difficult security areas, giving the army increased logistical flexibility.

Why is the presidential election of 1994 considered a second benchmark in the democratic transition?

In the presidential race of 1988, Cuauhtémoc Cárdenas clearly demonstrated that despite a highly fraudulent election he could win at least 37 percent of the vote, suggesting that the next presidential election in 1994 would become a test of whether or not Mexican voters would rally behind an appealing opposition candidate. In 1994, the three leading parties were the Institutional Revolutionary Party (PRI), which chose Luis Donaldo Colosio, Salinas's secretary of social development, former president of PRI, and a past member of the Chamber of Deputies and the Senate (and the first PRI candidate in thirty years to have held elective office); the Party of the Democratic Revolution (PRD), which ran Cuauhtémoc Cárdenas for his second attempt at the presidency; and the National Action Party (PAN), which chose Diego Fernández del Cevallos, a federal deputy, a member of the PAN National Executive Committee, and a leading lawyer. The PRI faced serious political difficulties after the Zapatista uprising (shortly after the race began) and, seven weeks later, when Colosio, the PRI candidate, was shockingly assassinated while campaigning in Tijuana. Confronted by a provision in the Constitution specifying when a candidate must resign any public office before his election, Salinas, with few supporters in the party apparatus, was forced to select Ernesto Zedillo, his former education secretary and Colosio's campaign manager.

However, the 1994 election took place under different electoral laws than did the 1988 election. These laws assigned sole responsibility for the election to the Federal Electoral Institute (renamed the National Electoral Institute), increased the election's transparency, employed international observers on Election Day, and received constant coverage in published public opinion polls. The election was considered by leading analysts to have been mostly free of fraud. Thus, 1994 became a test of whether the PRI could maintain its incumbent status or the opposition could succeed in defeating Zedillo. Citizens' beliefs in the fairness and importance of the election, given the political instability brought on by the Zapatista uprising and the assassination of the PRI candidate, were demonstrated on Election Day. The turnout of registered voters, 78 percent, was the highest recorded before or since. The PRI won with 50 percent of the vote, surprising analysts, and the PAN replaced the PRD as the second most important party, winning 26 percent of the vote. The elections demonstrated the competitiveness of the parties and confirmed citizens' beliefs that they were fair. However, the PRI actually benefited from the perceived political instability among some voters, who preferred to vote for the incumbent party rather than face a drastic change in leadership. The strong showing of the opposition parties in the Chamber of Deputies produced further electoral reforms that guaranteed an even playing field in the 2000 presidential election, where the opposition finally won with a plurality of votes. (For personal insights from this campaign, see the interview with the Labor Party candidate in 1994, Cecilia Soto González, at latinamericanhistory.oxfordre.com/page/videos/.)

What was the role of the Catholic Church in the 1994 presidential race?

No institution has been as significantly ignored by analysts for its role in the transformation of the Mexican electoral process specifically and the democratic transition broadly than the Catholic Church. In spite of important inroads by evangelical Protestants in the 1980s and 1990s, 85 percent of the population still identifies itself as Catholic. The majority of Catholics attend mass. More important, the Mexican public, in survey after survey, consistently grants the Church as an institution, along with educational institutions and schoolteachers, its highest level of confidence. Some Mexicans even expect the Catholic clergy to take positions on nonspiritual matters, including secular social, economic, and political issues. Thus, the clergy, through public statements and their involvement in religiously affiliated organizations that claim the largest membership of any type of organization in Mexico, including labor unions, have a broad impact on Mexican political values and preferences.

The 1917 Constitution strictly prohibits ministers representing any religion from using the pulpit to promote partisan political preferences. This prohibition is rarely violated in practice; instead the Catholic hierarchy since the 1980s has issued important public statements through individual dioceses advocating civic responsibility in exercising the right to vote and reinforcing the Church's support for democratic institutions and free elections. As public interest in the 1994 election grew, the Catholic Church took a proactive stance by advocating that each Mexican had a personal responsibility to vote. Indeed, it went so far as to say that registered voters who were not exercising their voting rights were committing a sin. We will never know for sure the extent to which Catholic bishops and priests influenced the turnout for the 1994 election, but there is no question that they did make a difference. They also played an important role in educating voters to judge candidates on their stated beliefs and credentials rather than on the basis of their party affiliation. Six years later, in the 2000 presidential race, they reiterated their position on the importance of voting, while simultaneously condemning as antidemocratic and sinful the tactics of candidates who used fear of change as a reason for maintaining the status quo.

What were the consequences of the assassination of the Institutional Revolutionary Party presidential candidate Luis Donaldo Colosio in 1994?

In late March 1994, well into the presidential election campaign, the Institutional Revolutionary Party (PRI) candidate, Luis Donaldo Colosio, was assassinated in Tijuana, Baja California. Since 1929, no Mexican president, presidential candidate, or candidate-elect had been murdered. Consequently, the death of Colosio came as a great shock to the Mexican public and political class, and was viewed as another destabilizing event coming on the heels of the violent uprising by the Zapatistas in the first week of January of that same year. Both events received significant attention from the international media as well as from Mexican domestic sources (see question on the presidential election of 1994 in this chapter). Colosio's untimely death had consequences for the larger electoral process and, equally important, for conditions inside the PRI leadership.

The broader impact was to reinforce the views of certain voters who were fearful of supporting opposition candidates in a time of perceived political instability. Such voters were more likely to cast their ballots for the replacement PRI presidential candidate, thus affecting the outcome of the presidential election and delaying an ultimate test of electoral democracy, that of transferring control from one political party to another. On the other hand, Colosio's murder led to decisions that made it obvious to all Mexicans and outside observers that the PRI's mechanism for choosing its presidential nominee was clearly authoritarian. With the election taking place the first week of July, President Salinas was forced to choose between the president of the PRI and the manager of Colosio's campaign, Ernesto Zedillo, a former member of the president's cabinet. The choice of Zedillo had several important ramifications within the party, all of which contributed to the democratic transition. Zedillo himself, after being elected president, did not resort to the dictatorial process used by all of his predecessors to designate his successor. Instead, he encouraged the party to develop a primary system to select its candidate, and for the first time in its history, in 2000, the party conducted an open presidential primary for its nominee, setting an example for other parties. Moreover, the designation of Zedillo, who had no prior history of holding party or elective positions, led to significant internal reforms within the party leadership, which wanted to promote PRI candidates boasting electoral and party credentials. Such credentials have since become the norm among the candidates of all three parties for governors and presidents.

How did President Zedillo contribute to the democratic transition?

Throughout his campaign, President Ernesto Zedillo, the last Institutional Revolutionary Party (PRI) president in the twentieth century, promised to strengthen the rule of law and, once in office, initiated important changes that affected the outcome of the 2000 presidential race. He used his executive authority in 1995 to carry out a series of significant reforms of the Supreme Court, Mexico's highest judicial body, and these became the basis for a more independent judiciary. He established a limit of fifteen years for justices serving on the court, or fewer if they reached mandatory retirement age. Under the reforms, the president would present a candidate for open positions, but a two-thirds majority of the Senate would have to approve his choice. Furthermore, as had often been the case previously, appointees were not allowed to have held a public office one year before their appointment. The reformed court could rule for the first time on the constitutionality of laws. Shortly after the new justices took office and the reforms were enacted, the court made several major rulings against the executive branch, demonstrating its independence.

Even more important for the democratic transition were changes Zedillo's administration instituted in the electoral laws, making the Federal Electoral Institute and Electoral Tribunal of the Federal Judiciary autonomous bodies and creating an even political playing field through public funding of all recognized political parties. In the elections for 2000, for example, the National Action Party (PAN) and its allies, campaigning on a joint ticket for president, actually received more funds than did the PRI. Zedillo also made a major change within his own party, instructing the party to create a primary system to select the PRI's presidential nominee, the first time in party history that the candidate was not chosen by the incumbent or former president. The PRI decided to institute an open primary where any registered voter could participate in the designation of its candidate. This is the only case to date among the three leading parties of an open, general primary for a presidential candidate. Finally, and perhaps most important of all, when the exit polls showed Fox the clear winner, despite the fact that the Federal Electoral Institute did not have the complete results, the president appeared on television to congratulate Fox, the PAN candidate, for his victory, legitimizing his victory before all Mexicans. Some analysts believe that, by doing so, President Zedillo headed off any attempt by PRI traditionalists to alter the electoral outcome. President Zedillo should be viewed as a president who encouraged democratic change and helped to legitimize a competitive, democratic process.

What is the Mexican bailout?

When Ernesto Zedillo took office on December 1, 1994, he and his economic team decided that it was necessary to devalue the Mexican peso against the dollar. During the Salinas administration (1988–94), the government had allowed the peso to become heavily overvalued. Zedillo's advisers recommended that Mexico allow demand for the peso in the international market to determine its value rather than peg it at a fixed rate against the dollar. Government economists believed that the ratio of the peso to the dollar would stabilize somewhere between 15 and 20 percent of its previous rate. Instead, international investors holding Mexican pesos or debt quickly began selling off their pesos, leading to a significant decline in its value. Before 1994, Wall Street firms had purchased large amounts of Mexican debt that were known as *cetes* because of their significantly higher returns than other comparable debt instruments. The unstable political situation in Mexico after January 1994 led most of these firms to pressure the Mexican government to issue devaluation proof bonds known as *tesebonos*. Many of these bonds were short-term issues, and $10 billion of them came due in the first two months of Zedillo's administration. Zedillo's government did not have sufficient reserves to pay off all of these obligations in such a short period, and investors began rapidly selling off the bonds. Mexico requested assistance and received a loan from the US Treasury and the International Monetary Fund. Ultimately it was able to meet its obligations, and it paid back the loan early.

In spite of meeting its obligations, Mexico experienced a general economic crisis as capital was withdrawn from the country, inflation increased significantly, and economic growth declined, leading to high levels of unemployment. Numerous companies went out of business, and interest rates charged by private banks increased dramatically. It took Zedillo's government two years under an austerity program to return Mexico to a high rate of economic growth. Nevertheless, many Mexicans suffered from the downturn in the economy.

PART III

MEXICO'S PRESENT AND FUTURE

10

MEXICO'S DEMOCRATIC CONSOLIDATION

POLITICS OF DEMOCRACY

Why was the 2000 presidential race essential to Mexico's democratization?

Democratic theorists argue that one of the ultimate political tests of a democratic model is whether national elections result in an alternation of those in power, especially in the executive branch, where most of the decision-making authority has resided in Mexico. Mexico's 1994 presidential election can be considered to have been competitive and significantly fair, but the incumbent party continued in office for seventy years. In 2000, the National Action Party (PAN) ran the former governor of Guanajuato, Vicente Fox, as its candidate. Fox represented an entirely new type of presidential candidate. He was the first PAN candidate to combine a successful political career at the national and state levels with a highly successful business career—as, in Fox's case, the chief executive officer of Coca-Cola of Mexico. Fox was a charismatic campaigner and broadened the appeal of the PAN well beyond its typical partisan supporters. The Institutional Revolutionary Party (PRI) ran Zedillo's former government secretary, Francisco Labastida, a career politician in the federal bureaucracy who had also served as governor of his home state of Sinaloa. Once again, the Party of the Democratic Revolution (PRD) nominated Cuauhtémoc Cárdenas.

Early in the race it became apparent that the presidential contest was between Fox and Labastida. As Election Day approached, polls indicated that the two candidates were neck and neck, the contest too close to call. But in the week preceding the election, when no more public polls were permitted, private polls revealed a significant shift among independent voters, favoring Fox. Scholarly polls and exit polls revealed that while Labastida outscored Fox on all other criteria, Fox exceeded Labastida significantly on one criterion: that of change. Thus, voters interested in change overwhelmingly voted for Fox. Mexico's 2000 election is a benchmark not only because an opposition candidate won the presidency for the first time since 1929, but also because voters believed that a change in leadership as well as a change in the political model was necessary. Fox generated high expectations about how change and a democratic government could improve the lives of all Mexicans. Younger Mexicans, in particular, were drawn to his message of change, the underlying basis of his campaign. The 2000 election results set in motion other underlying reforms that reinforced democratic governance, while at the same time created expectations the Fox administration could not fulfill, leaving an increasing number of Mexicans dissatisfied with democratic governance. When Fox won the election, 59 percent of Mexicans thought Mexico was a democracy. By 2013, only 47 percent believed that was the case. Even more important, the percentage of Mexicans who believed democracy was preferable to any other form of government had declined from 49 percent in 1995, when the Latinobarómetro survey first asked this question, to only 37 percent, the lowest figure in Latin America. Furthermore, 51 percent of citizens agreed with the statement that a democratic model was no better than a nondemocratic model or that an authoritarian model was preferable to a democratic one. Accompanying Mexicans' changing views of democracy was an increased level of intolerance for fellow citizens' political rights and beliefs.

Who is Vicente Fox?

Vicente Fox is a unique figure in Mexican politics. He grew up in Guanajuato, a state in west-central Mexico, within a successful farming family. He spent a year as a high school student in the United States, where he perfected his English. After attending Jesuit-run schools in Mexico, including the Ibero-American University (he was the first president since 1929 to graduate from a religiously affiliated college), he became a salesman for Coca-Cola of Mexico. He gradually rose through the ranks of the company and was eventually named the chief executive officer. He became the first president to have held a significant corporate position and the first to have worked for an internationally affiliated firm. Fox developed a serious interest in politics during the 1988 election, when he ran for Congress and was a supporter of the National Action Party (PAN) presidential nominee, Manuel Clouthier, who shared many of Fox's personal and career credentials. Fox, who considers himself to have been a disciple of Clouthier, won a congressional seat.

In 1989, he ran on the PAN ticket for governor of his home state. After an election characterized by fraud and public protests, President Salinas intervened, designating another PAN politician as governor. Six years later, Fox ran again, winning the election. He used his years as governor to demonstrate his political skills and to achieve support among PAN partisans and political leaders as a potential presidential nominee for the 2000 election. Considered an outsider because he had little experience inside the party bureaucracy, Fox created his own organization, Amigos de Fox (Friends of Fox), to cultivate and attract independent as well as PAN voters to finance his race for the presidency. He won his party's nomination and defeated the Institutional Revolutionary Party (PRI) in the 2000 presidential election. In retrospect, Fox can be seen as a highly successful campaigner who was much more successful winning office than governing. He appealed directly to his popular constituency rather than mastering the intricacies of governing, leaving office with many of his major proposals unfulfilled.

What was the Transparency Law?

When Vicente Fox became president of Mexico, on December 1, 2000, many Mexicans had expectations that a democratically elected government would be more accountable and transparent than past governments. Indeed, a genuine democracy incorporates the practice of transparency, which makes the government accountable to the people. A number of interested nongovernmental organizations (NGOs) worked with the executive branch to craft a new law that would require all federal executive branch agencies to provide information on request, as long as it met certain requirements and fell within the purview of the agency. For example, personnel files or information that would compromise national security would not be accessible. The law could be considered similar to the Freedom of Information Act in the United States. On June 3, 2002, the Transparency of Access to Public Government Information law was enacted, and one year later it was implemented. Its passage was considered a milestone by many groups. It established an independent agency, the Federal Institute for Access to Public Information (IFAI), to implement the program.

One of the limitations of the legislation is that federal institutions are required only to provide information that is already available in an existing document, rather than to create a document with new information. Nevertheless, many agencies have created new documents to provide requested information. Critics allege that some agencies are not forthcoming in providing relevant information or adequate answers to appropriate questions. Sometimes the answers to the same questions may be different. In the first five years of the IFAI's existence, from 2003 to 2008, more than 350,000 requests were processed. State-level agencies were also created between 2002 and 2006, and some included broader coverage. The more competitive the local political climate, the more likely the law was passed. One of the strengths of Mexico's transparency program is its accessibility. The IFAI encourages individuals to use the Internet to make requests. Such requests are recorded online, and both the requests and the answers are available to anyone who wishes to search a specific agency's responses or a specific subject matter. Furthermore, the IFAI requires that the appropriate agency respond to a request in a short period of time (thirty business days), and although an agency may request an extension, it will be granted the extension for only several weeks. In 2014, Congress passed a number of major reforms, making this agency the only one in the world with constitutional authority. Among the most important changes was an increase in the number of institutions subject to the transparency requirements, including political parties, NGOs, unions, corporations, and individuals who received public funds. Only the presidency can appeal a decision by the IFAI, and only on the grounds of protecting national security.

What is "Amigos de Fox"?

When Vicente Fox decided to become a candidate for his party's nomination for the presidency, he created an organization to enhance both his nomination prospects and his prospects of winning the general election. Established in 1999 by a close friend, Amigos de Fox (Friends of Fox) became a critical non-profit organization for raising funds for his campaign and for attracting supporters. Fox was the candidate of the Alliance for Change, which included the National Action Party (PAN) and Mexico's green party (Green Ecological Party of Mexico, PVEM). He was also supported by the candidate of the defunct Authentic Party of the Mexican Revolution (PARM). Traditionally, prior to 2000, the PAN had a small partisan base among likely voters in Mexico. Most surveys during that

period indicated that 20–25 percent of the voters could be considered core partisan supporters of the PAN. Consequently, no
presidential candidate from the PAN could hope to win the
election without strong support from independent voters, as
well as voters defecting from some of the other major parties.
Analysts believe the Amigos de Fox organization was essential to the electoral victory of Fox, who defeated the candidate
of the Institutional Revolutionary Party (PRI) by winning 43
percent of the national vote. Some observers believe that as
many as four million individuals joined Amigos de Fox. After
the election, the leaders of the organization were accused of
accepting illegal contributions from abroad and from Mexico.
The PAN was eventually fined $50 million for these violations.

What was the role of the private sector in the democratic consolidation?

During the 1980s and 1990s, when the democratic transition reached its apex, the Mexican private sector underwent
a shift in attitude toward partisan politics. In the preceding decades, the private sector rarely became involved in
opposition electoral politics. Most businesspeople who were
involved typically provided free or discounted logistical support for Institutional Revolutionary Party (PRI) campaigns.
Larger businesses pursued a neutral policy during elections
because they were afraid of reprisals from the government if
they openly supported candidates opposed to PRI. Some of
the private sector interest group organizations began urging
their members to take a more proactive and assertive role in
supporting their personal choices for public office. The most
influential business organization that encouraged its members to pursue such a strategy was the Mexican Association of
Businessmen (Coparmex), the independent business organization in Mexico with the largest membership. Similar business
organizations were part of the government-controlled corporatist system that required businesses with a certain number

of employees to belong to government-created organizations. Coparmex had been founded in Monterrey, the most important industrial center outside of Mexico City and the site of numerous global, capital-intensive industries.

The Coparmex leadership pursued two complementary strategies in the late 1980s. It persuaded businesspeople in their local communities to run for public office, first as mayors, then as governors. Typically, these individuals were active leaders of the local Coparmex branches as well as other business organizations such as the Chamber of Commerce. As these nonprofessional politicians increasingly succeeded as candidates of the National Action Party (PAN), they introduced changes in the party as well as in the electoral arena. The PRI itself, emulating the PAN, began identifying respected business leaders and nominating them to run for public office. The success of these individuals led to other business leaders providing financial support for local campaigns, an essential element in leveling the electoral playing field against the PRI. The efforts of the business community helped bring about electoral competition sooner than would otherwise have been the case.

What are the most important interest groups?

In many countries with an electoral democracy and a capitalist economic system, certain actors have a large role, or aspire to have one, in shaping public policy. In Mexico, the most influential institutional groups are the leading business organizations, some of the labor unions, and, indirectly, the Catholic Church. The group that exercises the greatest impact on public policy, specifically in the economic arena, is the Mexican Council of Businessmen, an elite self-governing organization of approximately forty-eight of Mexico's leading capitalist families. This small group of individuals meets regularly with members of the economic cabinet and occasionally with presidents. The reason for its influence on government policy is that the combined business interests of its members account for the majority of the largest publicly held companies in Mexico. In 2009, they controlled 27 percent of Mexico's gross domestic product. Most Mexicans have never even heard of this organization, which has been expressing its views collectively and individually since it was founded in the 1960s. One of the most serious criticisms of Mexico's economy has been the continued presence of monopolistic control in numerous economic sectors, such as telecommunications and television. One of the goals in the Pact for Mexico was to break up economic monopolies. In 2015, the government introduced significant changes in the telecom sector, but as of that date, control over the television sector had remained largely unaffected.

In the past, Mexican unions were important for sustaining the vote-getting ability of the Institutional Revolutionary Party (PRI). But as the democratic transition began taking hold, some unions became increasingly independent of the party and the government. The largest and most important union today is the National Teachers Union (SNTE). The SNTE effectively used the union's clout to create its own political party, forming political alliances with the National Action Party (PAN) to obtain representation in the Chamber of Deputies. It became a decisive contributor to Felipe Calderón's electoral victory in 2006. The union was so powerful that it also blocked necessary and long-overdue reforms to the educational system, especially in the hiring and firing of teachers. Consequently, early in his administration, President Peña Nieto arrested its leader, Esther Elba Gordillo, and as part of the Pact for Mexico implemented major education reforms, eliminating union control over the hiring and retaining of teachers, which were among a group of broader changes designed to improve the quality of the public education system and the long-term skills and training of the workforce.

Finally, there exist other actors that tend to exercise an indirect rather than a direct influence on public agencies. The most important independent institution is the Catholic Church, which plays an important political role, such as reinforcing the democratic transition and electoral process, and takes strong positions on social and moral issues, such as abortion. This does not mean that it has been able to block legislation at the local or state level that is contrary to its moral positions, such as that on abortion, but the executive branch is cognizant of its potential influence over the laity in many areas. The Church also has had a direct bearing on political issues, taking, for example, an assertive public position against Vicente Fox's administration when it attempted to bring a legal suit against Andrés Manuel López Obrador as a means of preventing him from running for president in 2006. The Catholic Church also played a significant role in supporting democratic political change in the 1980s and 1990s, by encouraging ordinary Mexicans to vote.

What was the role of the media in the process of democratic consolidation?

The Mexican media has become a critical voice in Mexico's democratic consolidation. The media increasingly professionalized its functions and goals, including the view that it should help educate Mexican citizens about their responsibilities as voters and participants in the democratic process, as well as undertake investigative reporting to ensure greater transparency and accountability among public institutions. The media has successfully carried out that mission, notably using survey research to convey public opinions on various policy issues and to determine voter preferences during and immediately before local, state, and national elections. Such polls were crucial to legitimizing and making possible Vicente Fox's victory in the 2000 election and to reinforcing the legitimacy of the Federal Electoral Court and the Federal Electoral Institute in its decisions concerning the narrow victory of Felipe Calderón in the 2006 election.

While the media continues to pursue an active role in investigating public malfeasance and other noteworthy subjects of interest to the public, it has become a victim of the power and influence exercised by Mexican drug cartels. The cartels have murdered dozens of journalists who have pursued stories about the cartels and their connections to political leaders. They have threatened publishers and reporters as well as their families. Mexico has become one of the most dangerous countries for journalists. These threats, combined with numerous assassinations and kidnappings, have made it impossible for journalists to investigate drug-related corruption. Such articles that are published rarely have bylines. This situation, which the government has failed to address, severely hampers the media in its efforts to enforce greater transparency and accountability, significantly weakening Mexico's ability to achieve a more complete democratic consolidation. (See interview with Ambassador Miguel Basáñez, an influential pollster during the democratic transition, at latinamericanhistory. oxfordre.com/page/videos/.)

What role did intellectuals play in Mexico's democratization?

In the twentieth century, intellectuals played a significant role in Mexico's political development. Many were precursors of the 1910 revolutionaries, and others joined the revolutionaries themselves in support of their social and economic positions. In the 1920s, one of Mexico's most prominent intellectual figures, José Vasconcelos, who served as education secretary in the first postrevolutionary government, abandoned government elites to become the first major opposition presidential candidate to run against the first formal candidate of the National Revolutionary Party (PNR, forerunner of the Institutional Revolutionary Party, PRI) in 1929. A number of intellectuals supported his campaign. In 1939, another leading intellectual figure, Manuel Gómez Morín, like Vasconcelos a former collaborator in the postrevolutionary governments, cofounded the National Action Party (PAN), which ultimately defeated the PRI for the presidency in 2000. But over the years, most intellectuals sought public employment either through government agencies and the foreign service or through major public universities.

Various intellectuals joined or were cofounders of smaller, short-lived political parties, particularly leftist organizations, but as a group, they did not have a significant impact on the democratization process until the 1980s. Their first notable public act in support of democracy took place in 1986, when many of Mexico's leading figures in the intellectual community signed a full-page announcement in the *Washington Post* denouncing widespread electoral fraud in the state of Chihuahua. A number of these prominent individuals were affiliated with two leading intellectual publications, *Nexos* and *Vuelta*, and published numerous essays and editorial pieces in these and other major Mexican newspapers and magazines advocating a democratic transition.

As the 2000 presidential race approached, a large group of influential intellectuals joined with other leading pro-democratic Mexicans from all sectors to form the San Angel Group, which encouraged opposition candidates to participate in the election, including Vicente Fox. Some of these intellectuals, including Jorge Castañeda and Adolfo Aguilar Zinser, following their own political ambitions, joined Fox's cabinet as the secretary of foreign relations and national security adviser, respectively.

FURTHER CONSOLIDATION

What happened in the 2006 presidential race and how did it strengthen Mexican political institutions?

As the 2006 presidential election approached, each of the three main parties nominated their presidential candidates. The leading candidate at the beginning of the race was Andrés Manuel López Obrador, the former president backed by the Party of the Democratic Revolution (PDR) who resigned his position as governor of the Federal District. He was the most widely recognized of the candidates and had developed a loyal following in the capital and the state of México. The National Action Party (PAN), the incumbent party, nominated a dark horse candidate, Felipe Calderón, after an intensive primary election. Calderón had served as his party's president and in Fox's cabinet. Finally, the Institutional Revolutionary Party (PRI), which hoped to make a comeback after losing the presidency in 2000, nominated Roberto Madrazo, the former governor of Tabasco and president of the PRI. As the campaign proceeded, Madrazo began to lose ground, and it became apparent toward the end of the race that the contest would be between the PAN and PRD candidates.

When the votes were counted, they revealed that Calderón had come from behind López Obrador, winning the election with a bare 0.6 percent of the vote, in the closest presidential election since 1929. Equally important, Calderón won only 36 percent of the vote, the smallest plurality of any presidential winner since 1910.

López Obrador immediately claimed fraud. He made a formal appeal to the Electoral Tribunal of the Federal Judiciary, the only institution with the legal responsibility for adjudicating disputed electoral results, and the court examined about 10 percent of the ballots. During an extensive investigation, described in a lengthy report, they found no evidence of fraud, but did identify and nullify a number of ballots for both candidates, which did not alter the outcome. López Obrador refused to accept the court's judgment, declaring himself president and encouraging his partisan supporters to boycott the government. Within a few months, despite his intensive efforts to delegitimize the government and the election itself, all but a small minority of core partisans declared their agreement with the court's decisions and their satisfaction that both the court and the Federal Electoral Institute that conducted the election were legitimate institutions. These results, despite the intense controversy, suggest there was support for the culture of law

and for democratic institutions, which contributed to the consolidation of Mexico's democracy.

Why did Felipe Calderón win the election?

Most analysts would not have predicted the victory of Felipe
Calderón in the presidential election of 2006 just a year prior
to the event. Indeed, when he received the nomination of the
incumbent National Action Party (PAN), he was the least well
recognized of the three leading party presidential nominees.
Moreover, many voters, including independents, who had supported his predecessor, Vicente Fox, were disappointed with
Fox's inability to produce significant changes as Mexico's first
opposition party president. Therefore, Calderón had to overcome the doubts of some of those voters in order to succeed.
On the other hand, Fox remained personally popular among
Mexican citizens, which helped to neutralize some of his administration's failures. As some observers noted, the 2006 election was the Party of the Democratic Revolution (PRD) candidate Andrés Manuel López Obrador's race to lose. To catch
up with and defeat AMLO, as López Obrador was popularly
referred to in the press and by the public, Calderón had to run
an aggressive campaign. Initially, he presented himself as a
social conservative. About halfway through the campaign, he
made a conscious decision to present himself as a centrist and
to reinforce those accomplishments, especially economic, that
could be attributed to Fox's administration.

As the campaign became more intense, Calderón and his
advisers decided to present López Obrador as a radical. They
even likened him to President Hugo Chávez of Venezuela,
who had alienated many Mexicans after criticizing President
Fox. Other groups, including private sector leaders, reinforced
this image in their own communications, including those on
the Internet. When one carefully examines the profile of the
Calderón voter, several significant characteristics emerge.
His typical voter was female, young—often younger than

forty-nine—fell into an upper-income category, was college educated, was a resident of the northern or central states (long PAN strongholds), was a resident of larger communities, was a Fox voter in the 2000 election, was a resident of states led by Institutional Revolutionary Party (PRI) and PAN governors, and was positive about Mexico's future economic situation. Calderón was also a stronger performer among those voters who identified themselves with the ideological center. Significantly, although López Obrador' placed the greatest emphasis in his campaign on social programs intended to alleviate Mexico's widespread poverty, Calderón received a large proportion of his own support from Mexicans who lived in poverty but who were beneficiaries of the antipoverty programs introduced by Presidents Zedillo and Fox. (For his own insights, see the interview with Felipe Calderón at: latinamericanhistory.oxfordre.com/page/videos/.)

Who is Andrés Manuel López Obrador?

Andrés Manuel López Obrador is one of the most influential and unique political figures in Mexico in the past decade. Born and raised in the Gulf state of Tabasco, he grew up in a modest family. At an early age he developed an interest in politics and became a disciple of a socially conscious Institutional Revolutionary Party (PRI) politician from his home state. After first pursuing a career in the government party and ultimately being blocked from advancing within that party, he joined the Democratic Current within the PRI and then the Party of the Democratic Revolution (PRD), and in 1994 ran as a candidate for governor of his home state against Roberto Madrazo, a leader of the traditionalist, antidemocratic wing of the PRI in a highly fraudulent election. In 1999, he took over the presidency of the PRD, and when elections were held for only the second time for governor of the Federal District, López Obrador won in 2000. As governor of the Federal District, López Obrador succeeded in demonstrating his administrative skills and his social and economic policy preferences. He introduced a number of innovative programs, including antipoverty programs designed to improve the economic status of Mexico's elderly population. He could be described as a populist with a charismatic appeal for many Mexicans. His constant exposure in the national media, which is centered in Mexico City, placed him in an excellent position to capture his own party's nomination, essentially without a formal election. Before López Obrador ran officially as a candidate, the attorney general of Mexico indicated he was going to bring a suit against him for violating a legal regulation he ignored as governor. Most observers viewed this decision as an attempt by the Fox administration to derail his presidential ambitions, since if convicted he would be ineligible to be a candidate. He received the backing of many Mexicans, as well as the Catholic Church, which openly stated that the public wished to consider him a viable candidate and demanded that the government drop its case. This controversy only gave López Obrador more notoriety, and the government withdrew its intention to prosecute him. Early polls showed that he was the most widely recognized presidential candidate in Mexico and the most popular among the candidates of the three leading parties. He failed to win the 2006 election, but he managed to shape the election. His refusal to recognize the election results as legal and his continued antagonistic behavior led to a decline in his popularity, even among many of his original supporters. Nevertheless, as the 2012 presidential race unfolded, he once again became the overwhelming choice of the PRD partisans, running against Josefina Vázquez Mota, the National Action Party (PAN) nominee and the first female presidential candidate from a major party, and Enrique Peña Nieto, the PRI candidate who defeated López Obrador with 38 percent of the vote (versus López Obrador's 32 percent). Again, López Obrador charged electoral fraud, ultimately leaving the PRD and forming his own party, the Movement for Renovation (Morena), which earned the fourth-largest vote (8 percent) in the 2015 congressional elections after the

PRI (29 percent), PAN (21 percent), and PRD (11 percent). In 2016, only 8 percent of Mexicans said they would favor the Morena candidate in the 2018 presidential election. The party performed poorly in the 2016 gubernatorial contests.

Why did the Institutional Revolutionary Party win the 2012 presidential election?

The presidential election of 2012 was held under new regulations introduced after the 2006 race. Those that may have had the greatest impact on the outcome of that election were the shortening of the electoral campaign to just ninety days and the strict enforcement of new rules governing the tone and content of campaign advertising by opposing political parties. The Institutional Revolutionary Party (PRI), which ran a distant third in the 2006 election, established itself as an early favorite, long before the formal process began. Strong support, in poll after poll, coalesced around the candidacy of Enrique Peña Nieto, the governor of the influential state of México, which borders the Federal District. Peña Nieto belonged to an important political family in his home state and was related to several previous governors and cabinet members. His popular support as a nominee and as a potential presidential candidate remained so strong that the leading opponent for the PRI nomination eventually conceded the nomination to him rather than hold a formal primary contest. The Party of the Democratic Revolution (PRD), which initially attracted several potential candidates, including a former governor of the Federal District, followed the same pattern, when it became apparent that Andrés Manuel López Obrador had overwhelming support from his partisans. The National Action Party (PAN), on the other hand, held an intensely contested primary, and a cabinet member from Calderon's government, Josefina Vázquez Mota, the first female candidate of the three major parties in presidential election history obtained the party's nomination,.

As the campaign began, Peña Nieto was well ahead of his competitors. As was the case in the previous two presidential races, economic conditions and personal security were paramount issues. In 2012, drug-related violence, including the dramatic increase in drug-related homicides during the Calderón administration, became an issue of even greater urgency. Recognizing its importance to likely voters, Peña Nieto promised to introduce changes in his antidrug strategy. Most notably, he indicated that he would alter the "kingpin" approach pursued by his predecessor, specifically that of trying to eliminate the top leaders of the multiple cartels and, in addition, would give more attention to other organized-crime activities, particularly kidnapping and extortion. Furthermore, he promised to introduce a new institution in the fight against the drug cartels, a gendarme unit, whose members would receive professional training from both the police and the armed forces. The philosophy behind this strategy was that Mexican security forces needed an organization that could perform police functions and tactics, while at the same time boasting military weaponry and training. He suggested that this new hybrid force would number some forty thousand individuals, but the gendarme unit he established once he became president consisted of only five thousand members and therefore would never be able to replace the armed forces in their multiple missions against organized crime. Some observers have suggested that certain voters may have found Peña Nieto an appealing candidate on this issue because under PRI administrations before 2000, the level of drug-related violence was much lower. Analysts have suggested that the PRI leadership handled its relationship with the cartels through informal arrangements and corruption, reinforcing long-standing patterns of stability among the leading cartels. Surveys suggested that a significant minority of Mexicans supported a government that would reinstate such an arrangement.

A careful analysis of the voting patterns reveals several additional insights into the outcome of the election. The most important explanation for Peña Nieto's victory is that, of all the candidates who had won the presidency since 2000, he needed to attract the smallest number of independent voters, or voters who had typically supported other parties, to win the election. For example, Fox and Calderón both had to double their partisan support to win. Furthermore, Fox, who was considered an outsider by most PAN activists and leaders, was victorious not because voters were attracted to the PAN's platform, but largely because of his personal appeal. A PRI candidate begins a presidential election with a distinct advantage over candidates from the PRD and PAN. The PRI has been able to maintain its strength because of the large number of core partisan voters, citizens who almost always support the party. The PRI has the largest contingent of partisan voters, followed by the PAN, and then by the PRD. López Obrador had to triple his partisan support in both 2006 and 2012 just to come in second place. In 2018, the year of the next presidential election, the PRD will be at a decisive disadvantage in this regard because its partisan voters, already fewer in number than those of the other two parties, will be split in two, with support going to Morena, López Obrador's party, and to the PRD. In 2016, a survey asking Mexicans which party they would support in 2018 revealed that 10 percent would choose the PRD and 8 percent López Obrador's party. The same survey showed that 22 percent would prefer the PRI in 2018, and 15 percent the PAN. It is also the case that the number of voters who report voting for the same party declined significantly between 2003 and 2015. Nearly half of the electorate, at the beginning of a presidential campaign, identify themselves as independent. Peña Nieto benefited from the fact that the PRI remains the most well distributed geographically in terms of grassroots support. He performed above his national average in three out of the four regions and, like his victorious predecessors, won the North, which typically provides a third of the votes for the presidency. Finally, the significantly shortened presidential campaign period and the candidates' sophisticated use of social media both played a significant role in the election. Although Peña Nieto, from the very beginning of the campaign, used Twitter and Facebook to attract supporters, a student movement, Yo Soy 132, which developed in the aftermath of an incident during the campaign, sought to support López Obrador and definitely helped close the gap between him and Peña Nieto in the final weeks of the campaign. Given the incomes and educational levels of typical social media users in Mexico, the influence of social media on presidential races will continue to increase, especially as a means by which voters themselves, and not just the candidates, will influence other voters (voters, unlike candidates, are not limited by the changes in the electoral law and may use social media long before the campaign period begins). One out of ten Mexicans reports using social media to access information about politics or to share it with others. Social media users tend to be more ideologically polarized, less trusting of institutions, and more supportive of democracy than those who do not use social media. Six out of ten Mexicans have access to the Internet; more than a third do so with their cell phones. Finally, if we examine the traditional demographic variables in the 2015 congressional election as a means of better predicting what kind of support each of the parties will attract in the future, it is clear that the PRI did especially well among older and less well-educated voters, the PAN appealed to Mexicans with higher levels of education, the PRD performance was the most well balanced among voters on the basis of gender, age, and education, while Morena strongly appealed to younger voters without any formal education. Surprisingly, the only party that voters perceived in a more positive than negative light was the PAN.

What is the National Electoral Institute?

The National Electoral Institute (INE), formerly the Federal Electoral Institute (IFE), is an independent agency established by federal law to oversee voter registration and all aspects of national elections. It was initially implemented in 1990 as part of a series of historic electoral reforms, but was incorporated into the Secretariat of Government, a politicized cabinet agency in the executive branch. In 1996, as part of a much broader and deeper reform to electoral laws, the IFE became a completely autonomous agency whose members are selected by Congress. It consists of a president and eight councilors. The regular members are elected for a term of nine years and may not be reappointed. The president is selected for a six-year term and may be reappointed. The establishment of an independent IFE was a significant step in convincing voters that the 1997 congressional elections and the 2000 presidential elections would be honest and transparent. Each state in Mexico initially had a local version of the IFE that was responsible for all state and local elections. However, changes in the electoral laws in 2014 assigned responsibility for state and local elections to the INE to eliminate inconsistencies at the regional level. If disputes occur over electoral results, candidates and parties can formally appeal to the Electoral Tribunal of the Federal Judiciary, which is the independent agency responsible for ruling on electoral disputes.

After their establishment, the most important electoral dispute was that of the 2006 presidential election. The candidate of the Party of the Democratic Revolution (PRD), Andrés Manuel López Obrador, disputed the honesty of the balloting that favored his opponent, Felipe Calderón, the National Action Party (PAN) candidate, who was declared the winner with a margin of only 0.6 percent of the vote. Before the election took place, the IFE garnered the highest level of public confidence of any government-sponsored agency, on a par with the positive attitude Mexicans expressed toward religious and educational institutions. In spite of the fact that nearly 30 percent of the voters initially believed there had been fraud in 2006, confidence in the IFE and the Electoral Tribunal of the Federal Judiciary declined only slightly. Within six months of the election, these two institutions regained their pre-election levels of confidence among ordinary citizens. Again, in the 2012 elections, when López Obrador disputed the outcome, these institutions were responsible for evaluating all claims of irregularities or fraud. The level of confidence in these two institutions contributed to the legitimacy of the decisions taken during both the 2006 and 2012 elections, and contributed to the institutionalization of democracy and democratic practices in Mexico. In the 2015 congressional elections, where the opposition PAN, PRD, and Morena parties, in addition to the much smaller parties, increased their representation over that of the incumbent PRI, the INE reinforced new electoral reforms, including one that allowed independent candidates to run for Congress, as well as for gubernatorial and mayoral positions. While it was praised for the integrity of the elections themselves, there were numerous accusations of vote buying or vote coercion before the elections. Despite widespread publicity, fewer than 1 percent of voters supported independent candidates, and most voters indicated that they wanted candidates with political experience. In the 2016 elections for twelve governors, numerous mayors, and state legislators, surveys revealed continued interest in independent candidates, but they did not perform well at the ballot box. There is little indication that voter behavior will be different in this regard in 2018.

What do the Mexican people think about the government's war on organized crime?

President Fox's increased efforts to destroy the drug cartels in Mexico met with strong public approval. He decided to significantly increase the role of the Mexican armed forces, given the inadequacies of local, state, and federal police in dealing with the cartels. The Mexican public has consistently maintained a high degree of confidence in the armed forces; thus, it was likely that Mexicans would view their use against the cartels in a positive light. By contrast, the police receive little support or votes of confidence from Mexicans. Fox had some success in his campaign against the major cartels, but Felipe Calderón decided to pursue them much more aggressively than any of his predecessors, arguing that the cartels posed an increasing threat to Mexican governmental sovereignty, national security, the rule of law, and general well-being. After 2007, drug-related violence and murders increased dramatically, but they declined in 2013, 2014, and 2015, and appeared to be on the rise in 2016. The Inter-American Commission on Human Rights reported that violence has contributed to a hundred thousand deaths in the past ten years. There are two related reasons for this. First, the government's strategy resulted in the arrests of a number of top cartel leaders, creating a vacuum in the leadership. Second, the drug cartels' violence was directed largely against each other in an attempt to wrest control of certain regions. Because the armed forces and the government federal police have taken much more aggressive actions against drug traffickers, cartels have killed many more representatives (and family members) of the military, the police, and the public prosecutor's office than previously.

In 2007, approximately 44 percent of Mexican municipalities had no homicides, representing a historic low in Mexico's homicide rate. From 2000 to 2007, fully 40 percent of all municipalities reported no murders. However, by 2012, only 30 percent of municipalities were murder free. Despite the fact that the overall number of homicides began to decline under Peña Nieto, the actual level and perceived level of criminal violence have produced a significant shift in public support for the government's strategy. Given the fact that the cartels rapidly began diversifying their criminal activities into such crimes as kidnapping, extortion, and human trafficking, it is more accurate to label them "organized crime." By 2010, more citizens believed the government would not be able to defeat organized crime than believed it could succeed. By 2015, however, 55 percent believed organized crime would win, while only 17 percent chose the government. By the fall of 2010, important institutions and the public increasingly expressed the view in polls or to the media that the government should consider other strategies to cope with drug traffickers, including negotiating with the cartels. Former presidents Zedillo and Fox have both called for the legalization of some drugs, believing that the interdiction strategy is not working in Mexico. The Mexican Supreme Court opened the door in 2015 for the legalization of marijuana for personal use in a decision that would allow a small group of individuals to grow marijuana. Uruguay has already legalized it. Since 1988, the National Addiction Survey has reported an increase in the number of Mexicans who have tried any illegal drug at least once, and marijuana accounts overwhelmingly for the most likely choice. Regardless of the court's decision and Mexicans' increased desire to try a drug, as well as overwhelming support (by seven out of ten Mexicans) for permitting the use of marijuana for medicinal purposes, Mexican public opinion is overwhelmingly (two-thirds) against legalizing marijuana. The governor of Guerrero, one of the states with the highest level of drug-related violence, in 2016 made the first serious public proposal to legalize the production of opium poppies for medical purposes. Peña Nieto sent a bill to the Chamber of Deputies in 2016 requesting legislation that would legalize marijuana for medical use, a decision that represents a significant change in the attitude of the presidency. The Catholic Church has also begun to express doubts about the wisdom of Mexico's war on drugs, as human rights violations by the military and security forces have increased significantly and the violence continues unabated. Complaints of torture more than doubled between 2013 and 2014, reaching 2,403. From 2006 through 2014, there were 11,499 complaints of abuse brought against the army and navy alone, and only 137 resulted in legal cases. For the first time, in an extraordinary admission, the Mexican secretary of national defense, General Salvador Cienfuegos, issued a public apology for the behavior of soldiers caught on video physically beating a woman lying on the ground. Bishop Salvador Rangel Mendoza of Guerrero even suggested that the governor's plan might offer a way out of poverty for many communities in his diocese. Nearly half of all Mexicans are afraid to go out at night, and one in four has stopped visiting friends or relatives.

What impact does the army's mission against organized crime have on civil–military relations?

Beginning in the early 1980s, under President Miguel de la Madrid, the government requested that the army take an active role in reducing the influence of drug traffickers in Mexico. During his administration and that of his successor, the armed forces largely confined their efforts to eradicating the production of drugs rather than interdicting drug dealers. By the time of the Zedillo administration (1994–2000), the executive branch believed it was necessary to ask the military to pursue a more direct strategy against the traffickers themselves in cooperation with US agencies, including the Drug Enforcement Agency and the attorney general. In return for taking a more active role in the pursuit of drug traffickers, the armed forces requested and received a more active voice in determining national security policy, as well as improved intelligence cooperation from Mexican civil agencies involved in combating the cartels, especially from Public Security and from the attorney general. President Calderón increased the armed forces' role even more dramatically after 2007, expanding to more than fifty thousand the number of troops and officers assigned to this task and sending mobile units to drug-related hot spots throughout the republic. A recent study of eighteen regions where troops were sent by the Calderón administration to counteract the cartels found that in sixteen regions, the presence of the armed forces did not reduce the cartels' impact.

The decision to increase the military's role was made by civilian authorities, including the president, but some analysts fear that in performing what are typically considered civilian police functions, the armed forces are further delegitimizing both the police and civilian institutions in the eyes of the Mexican public. Numerous active-duty officers and retired officers have taken posts in security positions at the state and local levels. On the local level, the media have reported friction between the army and civilian police, usually arising from actions by corrupt local police officials. Government officials argue that they have no choice but to assign the military to this task until an adequate civilian police force at the state and national levels can be created. During the 2012 presidential race, Enrique Peña Nieto, the candidate of the Institutional Revolutionary Party (PRI), suggested that he would reduce the military's drug enforcement mission, specifically by introducing a gendarme unit, a hybrid force trained in police and military skills. Although it was suggested that this unit would be composed of some forty thousand individuals, ultimately only five thousand were trained and began field operations in 2014. Efforts have been under way to implement professionalization and vetting processes for years, but to date these programs have not been successful in eliminating corruption or in replacing the military in fighting the cartels.

How do Mexicans define democracy and how committed are they to democratic governance?

In the past ten years, new survey research by academics and the media has made it possible to better understand how Mexican citizens conceptualize democracy and what this might mean for Mexico's ability to achieve a consolidated, liberal democracy. The initial results of two surveys that were supported by the Hewlett Foundation suggest several important ways in which Mexicans' view of democracy differs from that of other societies. First, and perhaps most important, there is no consensus among Mexicans as to what democracy means. For example, does democracy mean liberty or social equality or progress? It would be easy to imagine that the less consensus that exists about its meaning, regardless of what that might be, the more difficult it will be to implement a democratic consolidation and agree on its procedural rules. Second, half of Mexicans who took part in these surveys were equally split between two views of what democracy entails: liberty and freedom, on one hand, versus equality, on the other. Other Mexicans viewed voting and elections, type of government, lawfulness, and progress to be components of democracy. To compare Mexican and US views, nearly two-thirds of Americans viewed democracy as defined by liberty, followed by only 8 percent who defined it as equality.

Mexicans' support for democracy is also affected by the way in which they conceptualize it. In the first two highly competitive elections where a party other than the PRI won the election, those of 2000 and 2006, Mexicans most likely to view their country as a democracy were those whose candidate won the election. Needless to say, the view that one lives in a democracy only if one's candidate wins an election provides little support, if any, for a democratic model. The surveys also showed, fortunately, that after a relatively short period of time, the percentage of Mexicans who viewed their country as a democracy in 2000 and 2006 eventually returned to pre-election levels. Finally, more recent surveys by the comprehensive Latin American Public Opinion project, which compares Mexico with other Latin American countries, also suggest that a sizable minority of Mexicans, who view democracy as defined by progress or equality, would be willing to return to an authoritarian model if their definition of a democratic political model did not fulfill their expectations. Indeed, only slightly more than a third of Mexicans actually prefer democracy to any other form of governance.

What do Mexicans expect from democracy?

When Mexicans began a period of democratic transition in the 1980s, the focus among political leaders, ordinary Mexicans, and scholarly observers was on elections and how fair and free they might be. Elections are the most common and basic process by which democracy is achieved. Having free and fair elections is a defining component of what many citizens, including Mexicans, believe democracy to be.

When Mexicans are asked what they expect from democracy, most say they expect it to offer economic and social benefits that would improve their standard of living and their quality of life. This expectation would be the same for other political models. These benefits from a democratic model are more important to most Mexicans than the degree of liberty and freedom it might provide, in contrast to the semiauthoritarian model that existed from 1929 to 2000. How Mexicans define their expectations of democracy affects their evaluation of governmental and presidential performance. For more than a decade, most Mexicans have viewed the country's most serious problems as economic. Indeed, if all the economic issues are combined, it can be shown that more than half of Mexicans consider economic growth, inflation, and poverty to be the number one issue, followed by personal security. In the 2006 presidential election, the two leading candidates, Felipe Calderón of the National Action Party (PAN) and Andrés Manuel López Obrador of the Party of the Democratic Revolution (PRD), were within 0.6 percent of each other when the votes were tallied. In spite of the fact that López Obrador heavily stressed the alleviation of poverty during his primary campaign, Calderón won the election. Many analysts believe Calderón won the election because a sizable percentage of voters whose economic circumstances were modest and who were beneficiaries of government antipoverty programs in place under the Vicente Fox administration, especially the former Oportunidades program, voted for Calderón. Thus, Calderón, as a representative of the incumbent party (PAN), benefited from the expectation that his new democratic government would improve the quality of people's lives. But in the 2012 presidential elections, it could be argued that nearly

an equal number of Mexicans evaluated democracy's performance on its ability to provide security and to eliminate criminal violence, an expectation that continues. Most important,
Mexicans' evaluation of President Peña Nieto's performance
depends more heavily on their perception of his administration's efforts to deal with the most pressing issues rather
than the actual status of those issues. For example, statistics
on economic growth are less significant than citizens' views
of what the government is doing to promote that growth.
Recent scholarship demonstrates convincingly that in Latin
America, including Mexico, citizens' perceptions that a government is performing well with respect to corruption, crime,
and the economy increase their belief that the government
is interested in what they think—that is, what scholars label
"external efficacy." Mexico and the United States rank near the
very bottom of all Western Hemisphere countries on this scale.

What is the Pact for Mexico?

During the era of the pre-democratic Institutional Revolutionary Party (PRI) in Mexico, there existed a long history of
national political pacts. They typically existed between the
PRI-dominated executive branch and the two most influential non-state actors, labor unions and business organizations.
In the 1990s, at the highpoint of the democratic transition, the
PRI for the first time in its history lost its ability to ensure a
two-thirds vote in the legislative branch, preventing it from
accomplishing constitutional changes. Consequently, the PRI
began negotiating with the opposition. In exchange for support on some legislative initiatives, it agreed to electoral legislation that paved the way for the 2000 electoral victory of the
National Action Party (PAN). The Pacto por México, or Pact for
Mexico, by contrast, is an extraordinary agreement expressed
in ninety-five initiatives that is deep, broad, and focused on
nearly all major political, economic, and social issues that will
determine Mexico's future. The presidents of the three major

parties, the PRI—Party of the Democratic Revolution (PRD), and PAN—and the president of Mexico, signed this agreement the day after Peña Nieto was inaugurated, on December 2, 2012. Every analyst of the government's failure to address critical issues will find most of them highlighted in this document, as well as concrete proposals to resolve them. The document discusses breaking up monopolies and increasing competition, expanding antipoverty programs, and increasing citizens' access to and level of education. It also addresses such difficult political issues as expanding and clarifying the state's role in human rights, nullifying special legal privileges (which goes back to the colonial era), removing the prohibition against reelection in the legislative branch (thus strengthening that branch in the decision-making process), and changing the Constitution to reduce the five-month lag between the election of a president and his or her inauguration. It also addresses numerous security issues in the public eye, as well as the rule of law and corruption.

During the first decade of the twenty-first century, Mexico failed repeatedly to seriously address most of the obstacles to long-term economic growth, legal reform, and democratic consolidation. In contrast, President Peña Nieto, whose staff worked assiduously for two months to negotiate the Pact for Mexico, created a vehicle for all three parties to benefit politically from these proposed changes. An examination of the off-year electoral successes of the PRI in 2003 and 2009 clearly demonstrates that opposition parties in the past, pleased with their performance, typically pursued a selfish strategy of going it alone instead of forming serious legislative alliances to address fundamental policy issues. By creating an agreement for which all parties can take credit, the Pact for Mexico made it possible for the government, as distinct from individual presidents (who are generally more popular than their administrations in Mexico), to meet citizens' expectations. The pact lasted for only fourteen months, yet it enabled the passage of such controversial reforms as altering the administration of public education; increasing competition in the telecommunications sector; introducing consecutive reelection in the Chamber of Deputies and the Senate, as well as among mayors (opposed by the general public); transforming the attorney general's office into an autonomous agency independent of the presidency; restructuring the Federal Electoral Institute to take responsibility over state elections (opposed by the general public) and renaming it the National Electoral Institute; and altering the long-standing constitutional provisions prohibiting foreign and domestic investment in oil exploration (also strongly opposed by the general public).

11

CULTURAL, ECONOMIC, AND SOCIAL DEVELOPMENTS

What are Mexican religious beliefs and religious relationships?

The World Values Survey, which is the most comprehensive global survey of citizen values and attitudes, clearly demonstrates that Mexicans view themselves as strong believers in God. Indeed, 98 percent said they believed in God, compared with 96 percent of Americans. Nine out of ten Mexicans believe that God is important in their lives and that they receive comfort and strength from religion. Mexicans are much more likely than people in the United States to consider religion important in their lives (see Table 11.1). Regardless of their beliefs and whether or not they attend religious services, three-quarters of Mexicans describe themselves as religious. This description might surprise some readers given the fact that much of Mexican political history in the nineteenth and twentieth centuries involved conflicts between church and state, and the suppression of the Catholic Church by the Mexican government. Nevertheless, with the exception of the state of Tabasco, where local suppression of the Catholic Church and all other religious institutions was extreme in the 1920s and 1930s, Christian beliefs are widespread throughout the country. Approximately 81–85 percent of the population is self-described as Catholic, compared with only 67 percent of the population in Latin America. Five to eight percent of the population

Table 11.1 Do Mexicans and Americans have similar attitudes?

Statement	Mexicans (percent agreeing)	Americans (percent agreeing)
Family is important in life.	99	98
Friends are important in life.	78	93
Politics is important in life.	45	53
Work is important in life.	96	82
Religion is important in life.	84	68
Most people can be trusted.	12	35
I am a member of a church or religious organization.	38	35
Protecting the environment is more important than economic growth.	63	37
Men have a greater right to a job than women.	17	6
Being a housewife is just as fulfilling as working for pay.	68	75
Men make better political leaders than women.	23	19
It would be good to have respect for authority.	83	55
Living under a democratic system is good or very good.	83	80
I have a great deal or some respect for human rights in my country.	49	62
I have a great deal of confidence in churches.	64	58
I would be opposed to having a neighbor of a different race.	10	6
God is important in my life.	92	66
Cheating on your taxes is never justified.	78	79
I am worried about a terrorist attack.	87	53

Source: World Values Survey, Wave Six, 2010–14.

is Protestant, most of these people falling into the evangelical category. Furthermore, more than 80 percent of Mexicans in 2015 reported believing in the Virgin of Guadalupe, Mexico and Latin America's most important patron saint, and nearly the same number of people pray to her. A tiny percentage of the population claims no formal beliefs or is atheist. Nine percent of the world's Catholics live in Mexico, which explains in part why Pope Francis visited Mexico for a week in 2016. Nearly half of all Mexican Catholics report attending church regularly, typically a much higher percentage than that of people who report regular church attendance elsewhere in Latin America, and three-quarters attend religious services once a month or more. A recent study indicates that one in five Catholics watches or listens to religious services on television, the Internet, or radio. Most Mexicans believe it is important to celebrate births and marriages during a religious service.

Religion, and particularly the Catholic Church, has become more influential in the past two decades, in part because a number of religious restrictions were removed from the Constitution in 1992. The Catholic Church views itself as providing leadership in spiritual matters, but it takes public positions on secular issues, including human rights, democracy, the economic welfare of the population, and what it considers to be moral issues, such as drug addiction and abortion. For example, Church leaders have been critical of the negative economic effects of the North American Free Trade Agreement on poor Mexicans. Recently, they also have raised concerns about human rights abuses by the armed forces in carrying out the government's antidrug strategy. About a fifth of all Mexicans expect the clergy to take public positions on important policy issues. Consequently, the clergy has the potential to influence public opinion. Recently, half of all Mexicans said they would heed the opinions of religious leaders regarding politics even though two-thirds of citizens believe that such leaders should not influence government. In 2016, Confraternice, an organization of eight hundred religious associations, reminded religious leaders not to violate Article 130 of the Constitution by giving partisan support to candidates or political parties. Such a violation could lead to a fine of 1.5 million pesos. Furthermore, the Archdiocese of Mexico City, the country's most influential diocese, issued in its official publication a strongly worded statement condemning the extent of organized crime's influence on the 2016 elections and the continued level of violence and assassinations of journalists, and expressing the belief that some of those upcoming elections would take place in locations that can be described as failed states. The degree to which parishioners translate their religious activities into political participation is affected by differences among local dioceses and parishes. Moreover, half of all Mexicans believe that politicians who do not believe in God are unfit to hold public office. Mexicans overwhelmingly believe their religious institutions provide them with answers to moral problems and meet their spiritual needs.

How is the drug war influencing cultural and religious behavior?

The increased drug violence in Mexico, both among drug cartels and organized crime and against the Mexican police and armed forces—and the horrific ways in which attacks have been perpetrated on many Mexicans—have had some unusual effects on music and religion. Mexico has a long tradition of composing ballads, or *corridos*, that interpret numerous aspects of social, economic, and political change. Students of music believe that *corridos* helped build popular support for the Mexican Revolution. Thus, it is not surprising, given the presence of drug-related violence and especially the impact of drug trafficking in rural Mexico, that musical groups would take up drug traffickers as a significant topic in their recently labeled *narco corridos*. Regardless of whether the songs valorize or denounce drug traffickers, some of the leading musical performers have become victims of kidnappings and murder. It has never been clarified in the media whether these threats and assassinations are reprisals against the singers who support one cartel versus another in their songs, or whether some of these individuals are linked to drug traffickers or their families. Mexican officials have been attempting to restrict or ban the performance of *narco corridos* on the air since 1998 because many songs glorify the traffickers. The government has put in place some restrictions on their performance on the radio, in nightclubs, and on public transportation. In November 2009, the police chief of Tijuana banned Los Tucanes, a popular group that performs *narco corridos*, after the lead singer yelled out to two cartel leaders during a concert, "Mob rules!"

In addition, a life of crime and the unpredictability of one's life in the context of numerous economic setbacks have an impact on religious beliefs. Most important, there is an increasing emphasis among drug traffickers and other Mexicans on nontraditional religious saints, such as La Santa Muerte (the Saint of Holy Death). They often look like skeletons draped in a black or darkly colored sheet, holding a scythe, a symbol of death. As Alma Guillermoprieto reported in several essays, such saints are viewed as authentic by many Mexicans, and newsstands even sell videos demonstrating how to pray to them. The patron saint of desperate causes, St. Jude Thaddeus, has grown in popularity as numerous cults have increased their influence. It is evident, however, that drug traffickers do not profess or practice traditional moral and spiritual Christian tenets but use perverted or unique religious practices in order to protect themselves. Nevertheless, scholars who study security issues have taken these new religious influences seriously, as shown by a study submitted to the US Naval War College. Drug traffickers have also increased their impact in some rural communities by donating money to build or refurbish churches, even though the Catholic Church has prohibited priests from accepting funds from traffickers.

What are Mexican attitudes toward gender roles?

Mexican attitudes toward gender roles have changed significantly since the 1990s. Male attitudes toward sexual equality
are more traditional than the views shared by Mexican women.
Women have increased their presence politically, having, for
the first time, voted in greater numbers than men in the 2009
national election. They also elected women to 117 seats in the
Chamber of Deputies in the 2015 election, or 39 percent of the
300 congressional districts, compared with just 52 or 17 percent
of the districts in the 2009 election. The remaining 200 positions
in the Chamber of Deputies, known as plurinominal deputies,
are allocated from regional lists provided by each political party.
Another 90 women were selected as plurinominal deputies in
2015, making a grand total of 207 women out of 500 deputies.
The secretary general of the Institutional Revolutionary Party
(PRI) came to the historic decision that half of all nominees for
3,400 elected positions at the local and state levels in twelve
states, excluding governors, would be women in 2016. The increased presence of women in national politics has shown that
they are different from their male peers. Women were much
more likely to have had legislative experience at the federal
and local levels, to have grown up in rural communities, and
to have more modest socioeconomic backgrounds. Mexican
women have also increased their presence in the workforce.
The greater percentage of women who are employed full time
outside of the home and who live in larger metropolitan areas
has altered Mexican views on family size, the importance of
marriage, and other social values related to gender. For example, 39 percent of Mexicans in urban settings believe that more
women influence men's votes than the other way around,
whereas in rural settings, the reverse is true. Three-quarters
or more of all Mexicans believe that the country should pass
legislation requiring equal representation of women and men
in Congress, the Supreme Court, the cabinet, and among ambassadors. In some cases, Americans and Mexicans share similar views. In a recent study, 48 percent of Americans and 40

percent of Mexicans said they believe women would make better economic leaders than men. On the other hand, 23 percent of Mexicans and 19 percent of Americans think that men would perform better as political leaders (Table 11.1). In general terms, nine out of ten Mexicans believe women should have the right to work outside the home. Nevertheless, biases persist. When asked if men should be given a preference for employment if jobs are scarce, 28 percent said yes, compared with half that number in the United States. Nevertheless, 96 percent of respondents in a recent survey stated that women should have the same rights as men. Nearly three-quarters of those who responded in this way believe that further changes are needed to accomplish such a goal. One such change is a 2015 ruling by the Supreme Court that required the police to reopen a case and investigate it "from the perspective" of femicide, or the murder of a woman by a man for reasons related to gender. In 2016, seven out of ten Mexicans admitted they have witnessed a woman accosted by a man verbally or physically on the street. Nearly nine out of ten citizens believe this behavior should be denounced. In Latin America, one out of four men approves of or condones violence toward a spouse. Fifteen percent of Mexican men fall into this category, placing them roughly in the middle range of the countries surveyed. Tens of thousands of women in April 2016 marched in twenty-seven states to demand an end to domestic violence and femicide. Despite positive changes in legislation, critics have continued to emphasize the lack of punishment for such crimes. (Data in this paragraph come from various surveys, including the World Values Survey, the Latin American Public Opinion Poll Project, and Mexican polling firms.)

Mexican attitudes toward marriage and gender roles have also changed. When asked if a marriage would be more satisfying if both husband and wife worked and took care of their home and children, three-quarters of all Mexicans responded positively. Interestingly, those percentages compared favorably with the responses given by British citizens. On the other hand,

40 percent of Mexicans continue to believe that a woman has to have children to be fulfilled, compared with just 15 percent Americans. One of the gender biases that has stalled changes in gender attitudes globally is that toward the education of males versus females. The traditional bias has always favored boys over girls. In Mexico today, 79 percent compared with 93 percent of US respondents disagreed with the statement that a university education is more important for boys than for girls. Only 20 percent of Mexican respondents agreed with that statement. Surprisingly, the proportion of those who disagreed was actually one percentage point higher than that of US respondents. Finally, there exists disagreement on whether men have greater opportunities to obtain better-paying jobs than do women. In the United States, for example, an overwhelming majority of people believe that to be the case. In Mexico, on the other hand, only 43 percent believe men have a better chance of receiving such opportunities. Regardless of the prevailing gender views, one in three Mexicans admit he or she personally knows a family member or friend who was discriminated against because of her gender.

How tolerant are Mexicans of minority groups?

One of the important ways in which we can understand a society's treatment of others who are "different" from the norm is to examine the level of tolerance among its members. Survey research has made it possible to compare countries across several measures of tolerance. One way to measure the long-term potential for increased tolerance is to evaluate the degree to which adults consider tolerance and respect for other people as an especially important quality that should be fostered in children at home. For example, in 2000, four out of five citizens of the United States and Spain said they considered tolerance to be important. Mexico scored at the 70 percent level, about the world average. The most common way that global surveys test adult tolerance is to ask respondents, from a given list of individuals, whom they would not like to have as a neighbor. The World Values Survey of 2000 found that, worldwide, 43 percent of respondents would not want homosexuals as neighbors, 37 percent would not want those who had AIDS, and 16 percent responded similarly about people of a different race. Mexico's responses to these three categories were 45, 34, and 15 percent respectively. But in the 2010–14 surveys, those figures declined significantly to 23, 16, and 10 percent, coinciding almost perfectly with the US responses in 2010: 23, 17, and 8 percent. Interestingly, nearly half of all Mexicans in 2015 supported accepting homosexuals in public office and in the army. In 2015 surveys by the Pew Research Center and Parametría, 43 percent of Mexicans said they supported same-sex marriages versus 57 percent of people in the United States. Despite the fact that these figures demonstrate the significantly different levels of tolerance in the two countries toward minorities and other social ills associated with minorities, they also reveal that in numerous areas the gaps are closing. The dramatic changes in attitudes toward same-sex marriage is reflected in President Enrique Peña Nieto's decision to initiate legislation in 2016 to amend Article 4 of the Constitution. The amendment reflected the Supreme Court's decision to "recognize as a human right that people can enter into marriage without any kind of discrimination," including "gender or sexual preference." The comparative data are revealing in other ways. In the United States, gender, age, levels of education, and income have little effect on individual responses to the race variable. In Mexico, however, low levels of education and income increase the favorable response to the questions dramatically. Age also affects Mexican responses, but an indicator of future treatment toward minorities is the fact that among the 16–29 age group there exists little difference between the Mexican and US responses. Younger Mexicans also express significantly more tolerance toward neighbors who have AIDS or who are homosexuals.

Many forms of intolerance exist in Mexico, just as they do in other societies. Among the most frequently mentioned examples are religious beliefs, sexual preference, and race. In the first government study of discrimination in Mexico in 2005, the secretary of social development reported that nine out of ten homosexuals, elderly, people with disabilities, and indigenous minorities considered themselves to be subject to discrimination. One in five indigenous Mexicans claimed they had been rejected for a job on the basis of race. Mexicans of African descent were not even analyzed in the study. Women were also discriminated against, but Mexicans singled out the four previous groups as most subject to discrimination. The most prominent symbols of the violation of the rights of women in Mexico are the unsolved murders of hundreds of women in Ciudad Juárez over more than a decade, a tragedy that has received international as well as national attention. In 2014, eight in ten Mexicans believed that their society discriminated against people on the basis of age, sexual preference, origin, social class, race, and appearance. Some changes have occurred in recent years. Mexico created a National Council to Prevent Discrimination, the first such federal agency, in 2003. The most tolerant setting for gays is the nation's capital. The local legislature passed a civil union law in 2006 and then, in 2010, legalized gay marriage. Most surprising, the Supreme Court, in a 9 to 1 decision, declared that state and local bans on same-sex marriages violated the Mexican Constitution.

Religious persecution has also been a serious issue in Mexico. Numerous conflicts occurred between evangelical Protestants and Catholic communities, especially in rural areas, from the 1960s through the 1990s. It has been estimated that by 2000, approximately thirty thousand Protestants were displaced or killed in these confrontations. There also exists a link between ethnicity and religious affiliation, since indigenous Mexicans are twice as likely as all other Mexicans to convert to evangelical faiths, and the geographic distribution of evangelicals is heavily concentrated in states with large indigenous populations. The intensity of such religious intolerance compared with that in the United States is suggested by the fact that 16 percent of Mexicans would not want a person professing a different religion living next to them, compared with only 3 percent of people living in the United States.

What is Mexico's impact on cultural trends in the United States?

Long before Mexican immigrants accounted for a large percentage of the US population, Mexico exerted an influence on US culture. Over a period of many decades, Mexico had a significant impact on US art and architecture. The most influential painters were a group of artists known as the "muralists." The muralists represented a significant socioeconomic artistic movement in Mexico during the revolutionary decade of 1910–20, when a number of painters viewed making artworks accessible to the public as a critical function of art. These painters believed that art should be viewed in public settings and on public walls and ceilings. Given the many economic, social, and nationalistic themes that emerged from the revolution, painters such as José Clemente Orozco and Diego Rivera began painting murals, using the fresco technique, with political and social messages. Their art was supported by the Mexican government in the 1920s, and both also created works in the United States. But perhaps the greatest impact of this movement outside of Mexico occurred in the United states during the Depression, when the Roosevelt administration employed artists to paint murals in train stations, post offices, and other buildings, sometimes using techniques they had learned in Mexico. Other Mexican painters, who joined their peers in the United States, added their own palette and flavor, including Rufino Tamayo, who for much of his career was better known in New York than in Mexico. The influence of architectural style, especially in housing throughout the Southwestern United States, can be found everywhere.

Today, the music, cuisine, and language of Mexico are having an enormous impact on popular culture in the United States. Foods served for breakfast, for example, have been revolutionized by Mexican influences, and range from the ever-present burrito to huevos rancheros. Mexican salsas of all flavors and composition are widely served at sports events, in movie theaters, and in homes. Multiple fast-food chains specialize in Mexican food. Grocery stores stock more items originating from Mexico than any other ethnic cuisine in the world, including beers, beans, hot sauces, peppers, and tortillas. Corona is the best-selling foreign beer in the United States. Mexican foods such as guacamole and caesar salad are so commonplace that they have lost their identity as Mexican cuisine. The use of Spanish words and Mexican slang is evident in everyday language in the United States; such terms range from "mano a mano" to "macho," "enchilada" to "margarita," and "rancho" to "hacienda." According to a Pew Center study in 2013, thirty-eight million individuals in the United States five years or older, the majority of them Mexicans, were speaking Spanish at home. Spanish is also the most widely spoken non-English language among Americans who are not from a Hispanic country. The size of the Spanish-speaking audience in the United States has also influenced the growth of coproduced or sole-produced Mexican films. The musical influence has kept pace with cuisine. In 2010, the *New Yorker* magazine ran an extensive article about Los Tigres del Norte, a musical group from San Jose, California, who represent the norteño musical style. They boast a huge following among music fans. Selena, who died two decades ago, has sold more than sixty million albums, including songs representing the mariachi and ranchera genres, and the number of copies of her posthumous bestselling album of all time, *Dreaming of You*, reached five million by 2015. Among young adults (eighteen to thirty-four years of age) who listen to the radio, Mexican regional music ranks seventh in popularity.

12

WHAT LIES AHEAD?

It is clear from the answers to the questions in this book that
Mexico faces many difficult challenges. Some of these are
long term, others more immediate. Regardless of which issues
one considers to have top priority, most will be affected directly or indirectly by Mexico's economy, by its economic and
geographic links to the United States, and by the ability of
its government to generate confidence in public institutions
through effective governance, transparency, accountability,
and the rule of law. The most important economic challenge
facing Mexico is therefore its need to increase the country's
economic growth while simultaneously reducing high levels
of poverty. The lack of consistent growth has plagued Mexico
for decades, especially since the early 1970s. A comparative analysis among leading Latin American economies and
Mexico clearly demonstrates that Mexico has fallen behind
countries such as Chile, whether in terms of yearly economic
growth or decreasing levels of poverty. There are numerous
reasons Mexico's economic achievements have lagged behind
those of Chile and other countries, including the lack of competitiveness in numerous economic sectors, the lack of labor
flexibility, the low levels of transparency, and the high levels
of corruption. Mexican leadership has continued to increase
federal funding for social spending, including its successful
Prospera (formerly Progresa, 1997–2002, and Oportunidades,

2002–2014) antipoverty program. Nevertheless, as unemployment increases because of poor economic growth, poverty levels will increase or remain stable. Mexico demonstrated under Presidents Zedillo and Fox that, like Chile and Brazil, it could reduce poverty levels, but it needs to reinforce those factors that will provide greater consistency in its economic growth rates. This pattern will be even more important in the next decade as the country's reliance on petroleum revenues for federal funding declines. These internal limitations and obstacles are under Mexico's control. But in spite of achieving a democratic electoral process and increasing the power of the judicial and legislative branches of government, it has not successfully addressed many fundamental economic issues. This is the case despite the Pact for Mexico's focus on competition, corruption, and educational reforms. The one significant economic variable over which Mexico exerts little influence is its economic relationship with the United States. One of the reasons Chile continued to boast higher economic growth is that it is not tied so strongly to the US economy and therefore has not been nearly as adversely affected by the recession and its aftermath in 2008. Long-term comparisons of annual growth of gross domestic product reveal that Chile averaged 5.2 percent from 1987 to 2016, compared with Mexico's 2.6 percent from 1994 to 2016.

The second issue that Mexico faces—and that receives far more attention from US policymakers and the media—is its security situation. In spite of increased cooperation between the United States and Mexico, assistance through the Mérida Initiative, the introduction of legal reforms, and the creation of a gendarme unit of military- and police-trained personnel, organized criminal activity continues unabated. Still, the incidence of homicides related to organized crime declined somewhat between 2012 and 2015, rising again in 2016. In fact, even though the number of homicides was lower for a brief period, the perceived level of violence increased. The Mexican public has become increasingly discouraged about actual and perceived levels of personal security. The kidnapping and disappearance of forty-three students from a teachers' college in southern Mexico in 2014, and the inability of the government to provide a transparent and convincing explanation for what happened to these students and who is responsible, only reinforce these perceptions and realities. Only one in four Mexicans believes that human rights are respected, and one in five that the law applies equally to all citizens. The majority of Mexicans believe that the government and specifically the president bear responsibility for ensuring these rights and improving respect for them. Since 2009, they no longer believe that the federal government can defeat drug-trafficking organizations and organized crime, even with the armed forces playing a leading role in the government's antidrug strategy. Indeed, that lack of confidence explains why a third of Mexicans have consistently supported intervention by US troops in fighting the cartels, on the condition that such intervention will reduce the violence. The increasing growth of organized crime and its expansion into other illegal activities, which can be aptly described as "economic diversification," ranges from kidnapping for ransom and control of overland undocumented migration routes to the United States to sales of illegal goods and products outside of drugs and to the widespread implementation of protection rackets that extort payments from small and large businesses alike. Citizens' attitudes toward these conditions have been translated into direct political behavior and explain the significant loss of the National Action Party (PAN) to the Institutional Revolutionary Party (PRI) and the Party of the Democratic Revolution (PRD) in the 2012 presidential elections, as well as the rapid decline in support for President Enrique Peña Nieto and the PRI since 2013. Mexicans view Peña Nieto's administration as performing badly in nearly all areas of public policy, but especially so in efforts to combat poverty, hunger, unemployment, corruption, crime, and drug trafficking. Currently, and for the past two years, President Peña Nieto has received the lowest ratings of a president from the public since 2000.

More important than its impact on these elections is the ability of the Mexican government to maintain sovereign control over public institutions at the local and state levels. Governmental sovereignty, personal security, and reduction of the presence and influence of drug trafficking and organized crime are all linked to Mexico's economic challenges. One of the reasons organized crime has attracted new recruits is the high level of poverty and the lack of economic opportunity in Mexico. These conditions were exacerbated by the recession in the United States before 2012 and the significant decrease in illegal immigration from Mexico to the United States. Between 2009 and 2014, more Mexicans left the United States and returned to their homeland than emigrated to the United States. Our own intelligence agencies estimate that approximately 450,000 Mexicans are employed in the drug trade. The United States, of course, exerts a far greater economic influence over this criminal activity and its growth by being the largest market for illegal drugs in the world, most of which are produced in or shipped from Mexico. These organizations are strongly linked to criminal gangs in the United States and in Canada, and consequently play a role in some US social problems. Mexico cannot adequately address its economic issues or its organized-crime issues without a proactive US strategy to reduce drug consumption and to increase its economic assistance for antipoverty programs in Mexico. It is critical to keep in mind that the poverty rate in Mexico in 2012 was the same as in 1994, but because the population has increased dramatically, this means that fourteen million more Mexicans are living in poverty now than twenty years ago. Both countries are spending most of their resources on the consequences of crime and poverty, not on the causes.

The third issue Mexico has to confront is the impact these and other conditions is having on democratization. Mexico is an electoral democracy; most observers believe it now boasts free and fair elections even if a significant minority of Mexicans express doubts about their fairness. On the other hand, Mexico has disappointed many citizens as well as analysts in their expectations of what a democratic polity would bring to the country and to its citizens. For example, one of the essential features of a functioning democracy is accountability and transparency. In 2003, President Fox oversaw the implementation of a new Transparency Law. This law requires all federal agencies to provide answers to questions posed by ordinary citizens, journalists, researchers, and others unless they infringe on personal, confidential information and national security. Thousands of requests have been made and answered. But since the implementation of the law, instead of broadening citizens' access and answering their questions, numerous agencies have increased their resistance to responding to all legitimate questions. Recent reforms have addressed some of these issues, and the Transparency Law has incorporated more institutions under its jurisdiction. It remains to be seen whether those changes will increase public access to both government and nongovernment institutions and, perhaps more important, increase their confidence in Mexico's transparency and accountability. Perhaps even more disturbing is Mexico's lack of progress on human rights abuses under a democracy. The government's antidrug strategy and its reliance on the armed forces to implement this strategy have led to a dramatic increase in human rights allegations and abuses. Yet the government's track record since 2000 in investigating the allegations and bringing charges against the perpetrators, often the armed forces, has been poor at best. For example, 9,644 complaints were made against the army between 2006 and 2014. Eight out of ten Mexicans currently believe that the government and organized crime are equally responsible for forced disappearances. Thus, it is no surprise that two-thirds of Mexicans express dissatisfaction with government efforts to protect human rights. The rule of law is one of the essential ingredients that defines a democratic society, yet the implementation of the rule of law in Mexico is seriously flawed in this and other, numerous respects. Indeed, victims of crime, or citizens who believe their personal security is threatened, are more likely to support infringements on the rule of law, such as vigilanteeism. This situation explains why half of all Mexicans today agree with the statement that they should establish their own police force to protect themselves from crime, rather than rely on their local government's institutions.

Mexico's failure to address these and the other pressing problems described in this chapter is disappointing to millions of its citizens. Many of the requirements of a consolidated, democratic model would be met if these issues were properly addressed. But the fact that they have not been resolved, as in many parts of Latin America, has caused Mexican citizens to question democracy itself as a political model. According to a 2012 survey by the Latin American Public Opinion Project, 19 percent of Mexicans approved "of people participating in a group working to violently overthrow an elected government." Mexico ranked near the top of Latin American countries, including Bolivia and Guatemala, in supporting this statement; Uruguay and Argentina ranked at the top in the percentage of respondents opposed to taking such radical action. Researchers believe that a respondent's willingness to support a violent approach depends on his or her own personal experience with corruption. Mexicans view corruption as a serious problem, and they see it as the primary cause of the government's inability to stop drug-related violence. Ironically, two-thirds of Mexicans are not familiar with Public Function, a cabinet-level agency that is the most important government agency in the battle against corruption. On the other hand, in 2016, scholars from two leading universities in Mexico City presented an initiative entitled Ley 3de3 (Law 3 of 3).The initiative, which garnered 120,000 signatures, asked that all candidates for elective public office be required to make public their financial assets, tax records, and any conflicts of interest. Three out of four Mexicans support this proposal, and most say they would not vote for a candidate who did not make this information available; half believe it would reduce corruption among politicians and public figures.

Mexicans, like most Latin Americans, are seeking a government that can produce concrete results in its efforts to deal with long-standing issues related to economic and social development, as well as to flawed government accountability and integrity. There are no short-term solutions. It is likely that the current dissatisfaction with the national government will translate in the 2018 presidential election into the PRI being replaced as the party with control over the federal executive branch. Regardless of which party has been in charge of the executive branch since 2000 and has had a plurality in the legislative branch, there exists little likelihood that it will have both the will and political skill to address these same issues more effectively than the incumbent government. The Pact for Mexico, from a legislative perspective, marked the most important collaboration among the three leading parties to address some of the underlying issues, but it lasted for only fourteen months. Whereas the federal and state governments require imaginative and collaborative legislation across parties, if such notable institutional reforms lack effective implementation or reinforcement by changes in behavior, they will not produce the desired outcomes. The capacity of the Mexican government to carry out its responsibilities and enforce laws is the lowest among the other Latin American countries that are viewed as having the highest capacity to perform these tasks. Regardless of which party is victorious in 2018, most of the issues facing Mexico in 2000 will still be at the top of the country's political and economic agenda during that election and throughout the next presidential administration.

CHRONOLOGY OF MEXICAN PRESIDENTS, 1964–2018

2012–2018 Enrique Peña Nieto
2006–2012 Felipe Calderón
2000–2006 Vicente Fox
1994–2000 Ernesto Zedillo
1988–1994 Carlos Salinas
1982–1988 Miguel de la Madrid
1976–1982 José López Portillo
1970–1976 Luis Echeverría
1964–1970 Gustavo Díaz Ordaz

SELECTED SUGGESTED READINGS
IN ENGLISH

Bailey, John. *The Politics of Crime in Mexico: Democratic Governance in a Security Trap*. Boulder, CO: Lynne Rienner, 2014.

Beezley, William H., ed. *Oxford History of Mexico*. New York: Oxford University Press, 2010.

Camp, Roderic Ai. *Politics in Mexico: Democratic Consolidation or Decline?* New York: Oxford University Press, 2014.

Camp, Roderic Ai, ed. *The Oxford Handbook of Mexican Politics*. New York: Oxford University Press, 2012.

Conger, Lucy. *A Mandate for Mexico*. Washington, DC: Woodrow Wilson Center, Mexico Institute, 2015.

Domínguez, Jorge I., Kenneth F. Greene, Chappell H. Lawson, and Alejandro Moreno. *Mexico's Evolving Democracy, A Comparative Study of the 2012 Elections*. Baltimore: Johns Hopkins University Press, 2015.

Domínguez, Jorge I., and Chappell Lawson, eds. *Mexico's Pivotal Democratic Election: Candidates, Voters, and the Presidential Campaign of 2000*. Stanford, CA: Stanford University Press, 2004.

Domínguez, Jorge I., Chappell Lawson, and Alejandro Moreno, eds. *Consolidating Mexico's Democracy: The 2006 Presidential Campaign in Comparative Perspective*. Baltimore: Johns Hopkins University Press, 2009.

Edmonds-Poli, Emily, and David A. Shirk. *Contemporary Mexican Politics*. Lanham, MD: Rowman & Littlefield, 2015.

González, Francisco E. *Dual Transitions from Authoritarian Rule: Institutionalized Regimes in Chile and Mexico, 1970–2000.* Baltimore: Johns Hopkins University Press, 2008.

Hernández Chávez, Alicia. *Mexico: A Brief History.* Berkeley: University of California Press, 2006.

Hughes, Sallie. *Newsrooms in Conflict: Journalism and the Democratization of Mexico.* Pittsburgh: University of Pittsburgh Press, 2006.

Krauze, Enrique. *Biography of Power: A History of Modern Mexico, 1810–1996.* New York: HarperCollins, 1997.

Lee, Erik, and Christopher Wilson, eds. *The U.S.–Mexico Border Economy in Transition.* Washington, DC: Woodrow Wilson Center, Mexico Institute, 2015.

Martí I Puig, Salvador, et al., eds. *Democracy in Mexico, Attitudes and Perceptions of Citizens at National and Local Level.* London: University of London, Institute of Latin American Studies, 2014.

Morris, Stephen D. *Gringolandia: Mexican Identity and Perceptions of the United States.* Lanham, MD: Rowman & Littlefield, 2005.

Mossige, Dag. *Mexico's Left: The Paradox of the PRD.* Boulder, CO: Lynne Rienner, 2013.

Organisation of Economic Co-operation and Development. *OECD Economic Surveys: Mexico.* Mexico: OECD Publishing, 2015.

Oxford Research Encyclopedia of Latin American History. "Democratizing Mexican Politics." Videos. (latinamericanhistory.oxfordre.com/page/videos/).

Peschard-Sverdrup, Armand B., and Sara R. Rioff, eds. *Mexican Governance: From Single-Party Rule to Divided Government.* Washington, DC: Center for Strategic and International Studies, 2005.

Rodríguez O., Jaime E. *The Divine Charter: Constitutionalism and Liberalism in Nineteenth-Century Mexico.* Lanham, MD: Rowman & Littlefield, 2005.

Selee, Andrew. *Decentralization, Democratization, and Informal Power in Mexico.* University Park: Pennsylvania State University Press, 2012.

Selee, Andrew, and Jacqueline Peschard, eds. *Mexico's Democratic Challenges: Politics, Government, and Society.* Washington, DC: Woodrow Wilson Center, 2010.

Thacker, Strom. *Big Business, the State, and Free Trade: Constructing Coalitions in Mexico.* Cambridge: Cambridge University Press, 2000.

Villiers Negroponte, Diana. *The End of Nostalgia: Mexico Confronts the Challenges of Global Competition*. Washington, DC: Brookings Institution Press, 2013.
Wilson, Christopher, Erik Lee, and Alma Bezares Calderón. *Competitive Border Communities*. Washington, DC: Woodrow Wilson Center, Mexico Institute, 2015.

INDEX

Note: page numbers followed by *t* and *m* refer to tables and maps respectively

abortion, 161, 185
Africa, Africans, 77
agriculture
  colonial period and, 72
  environmental concerns in,
    35–37, 55–56
  and the evolution of modern
    political structures, 118, 136
  expansion of, 56, 86
  Mexican Revolution and, 95–97
  Mexico's democratic transition
    and, 135–37
  nationalization of, 126
  US-Mexican relations and,
    113, 136
  See also land, land ownership;
    peasants; Procampo
Aguilar Zinser, Adolfo, 163
Alemán generation, 115–16, 138
Alemán, Miguel, 115–16, 118
  civilian supremacy and, 114
  and the evolution of modern
    political structures,
    114, 125–26
Alliance for Change, 157
Alvarez, Juan N., 82
Anti-Reelectionist Party, 91.
  See also Madero, Francisco I.

Archdiocese of Mexico City, 186.
  See also Catholic Church;
    Mexico City
Archduke Maximilian, 82
architecture, 194. *See also* culture
Argentina, 29, 42
Arizona, 8, 49, 59
  immigration and, 53–55
  Mexican-American War and, 80
art, arts, 50–52, 102–4, 186–87,
    193–95. *See also* architecture;
    culture; literature;
    muralists; music
asset poverty, 21. *See also* poverty
AUC. *See* United Self Defense of
    Colombia
austerity measures, 128–29.
  See also economics, economy
Autonomous Technological
    Institute of Mexico
    (ITAM), 130
Ávila Camacho, Manuel, 44, 108,
    114, 116–17
Azuela, Mariano, 103

Bank of Mexico, 58, 106
banks, banking
  crisis in the, 127

Mexico's democratic transition
and, 136–37
nationalization of, 31, 127, 136
See also economics, economy
BBVA Bancomer, 52
Beltrán Leyva Organization, 7, 13.
See also drug cartels
Benito Juárez Anti-Reelectionist
Club, 91
Bolivia, 201
Border 2012 Program, 36–37
Brazil
comparisons between Mexico
and, 42, 197
World War II and, 112
Bush, George H. W., 47, 136.
See also United States
Bush, George W., 26, 54. *See also*
United States
business, businesses
current state of, 10, 19,
28–31, 198
and the evolution of modern
political structures, 31
Mexico's colonial heritage
and, 75–77
Mexico's democratic
consolidation and, 158–59
Mexico's democratic transition
and, 180–82
Mexico's semi-authoritarian
model and, 98–99, 110–11,
126–27, 180
NAFTA and, 25–28, 32–34
organizations, 98, 110, 127, 140,
158–59, 180
petroleum industry
and, 30, 111
See also competition,
competitiveness; economics,
economy; monopolies

Cabañas, Lucio, 123. *See also*
guerrilla groups

Calderón, Felipe, 4–5, 7, 9–10, 36,
66, 138, 203
drugs and, 4, 174, 176
Mexico's democratic
consolidation and, 164
Mexico's economic model
and, 31
poverty and, 179
election win of, 160, 165–66, 172
California, 53, 59
Mexican-American War and, 80
US-Mexican relations and,
56, 59, 80
Calles, Plutarco Elías
and the evolution of modern
political structures, 98,
104–7, 114
Mexican Revolution and, 79,
106, 109
PNR and, 44, 98, 105
See also politics
Camacho, Manuel Avila, 44, 108,
114, 116–17
Canada, 14, 33, 47, 49, 59–60
drugs and, 5, 8
NAFTA and, 26–27
Cananea Consolidated Copper
Co., 49
capabilities poverty, 21. *See also*
poverty
capitalism, 30–34
Mexico's democratic
consolidation and, 158–59
Mexico's economic model
and, 30–32, 86–88
state, 87–88
See also economics, economy;
entrepreneurial families;
entrepreneurs
Cárdenas, Lázaro, 109–10, 112,
119, 126
and the evolution of modern
political structures, 105,
108–10, 114, 132–33

Mexican Revolution and, 98
  petroleum industry and, 111–12
  PNR and, 44, 98
  See also politics
Cárdenas Solórzano,
    Cuauhtémoc, 133–35, 153
  electoral strength of, 120, 133
  Mexico's democratic transition
    and, 121, 143
  See also politics
Carranza, Venustiano, 43, 93–95,
    100, 113. *See also* politics
cars, 34–35. *See also* environmental
    issues; pollution
Castañeda, Jorge, 163
Catholic Church, 159, 167, 183–87
  1994 presidential election and
    the, 43, 144–45
  Constitutions and the,
    73–74, 106
  drugs and the, 175, 186–87
  and the evolution of modern
    political structures, 43,
    131, 144–45
  land ownership and the,
    71–75, 81–82
  Liberal-Conservative conflicts
    and the, 73–74, 79
  Mexico's colonial heritage and
    the, 69–74
  Mexico's democracy and the,
    84–85, 131, 160–61
  public opinion on the, 184*t*
  relations between state and the,
    71–74, 106–7, 183–86
  and the War of the
    Reform, 81–83
  See also religion
Celaya, Battle of, 93
CEMLA. *See* Economic
    Commission for Latin
    America
CEN. *See* National Executive
    Committee

Chamber of Deputies, 120, 124,
    143–44, 160, 175, 182, 188.
    See also Congress, Mexican;
    plurinominal system;
    politics; Senate
Chávez, Carlos, 104
Chávez, Hugo, 165
Chiapas, 26, 62–64, 122, 140
Chicago Council on Foreign
    Relations, 26
Chihuahua, 6–7, 13, 163
Chile, 29, 42, 196
China, 29, 49, 59–60
Cienfuegos, General Salvador, 175
Ciudad Juárez, 7, 11, 56, 92–93,
    192. *See also* El Paso, Texas
Clemente Orozco, José, 102, 193.
    See also art, arts
Clouthier, Manuel, 155
CNC. *See* National Peasant
    Federation
CNOP. *See* National Federation of
    Popular Organizations
Coca-Cola of Mexico, 153, 155. *See
    also* Fox, Vicente
Colombia, drug trafficking
    in, 11, 13. *See also* drug
    cartels; drugs
Colorado, 80
Colosio, Luis Donaldo, 143
  assassination of, 145–47
  candidacy of, 143
Comonfort, Ignacio, 82
competition, competitiveness,
    25–26, 28–29, 33, 130–31.
    See also business, businesses;
    economics, economy
Confraternice, 185
Congress, Mexican, 15, 86, 134
  elections of 2015 of the,
    171, 173
  electoral reforms and the,
    38–39, 116–17, 120, 123–25,
    144, 172–73

and the evolution of modern
political structures, 98,
104–26, 172
Mexico's democracy and, 39,
42–44, 64, 87, 124, 146
See also Chamber of Deputies;
politics; Senate
Congress, US, 15, 80
immigration and, 52–55
NAFTA and, 136
See also politics
Conservatives
conflicts between Liberals and,
73–74, 78–88
Mexico's colonial heritage
and, 78–79
and the War of the
Reform, 81–83
See also Liberals, Liberal party;
politics
Constitution, US, 101
Constitutionalist Army, 93, 99,
106. *See also* Villa, Pancho;
Wilson, Woodrow
Constitutions, Mexican
of 1857, 74, 79, 83–85
of 1917, 30, 74, 79, 83–89, 92,
100–6, 110, 145
Catholic Church and, 79, 185–86
and the evolution of modern
political structures,
83–85, 104–10
Mexican Revolution and, 79,
85, 100–2
Mexico's democratic transition
and, 143–45
and the principle of
constitutionalism, 100–1
reforms to the, 79, 82–85, 181
See also Mexico, Mexicans;
politics
Convention of Aguascalientes, 93

Coparmex. *See* Mexican
Association of Businessmen
corridos, 186. *See also* culture; *narco
corridos*
corruption, 18–19, 28
drugs and, 11–12, 162, 169
future and, 198–200
Mexico's democratic
consolidation and, 173,
177, 181
public opinion on, 180
See also crime; drug
cartels; drugs
Costa Rica, 113
Council of the Indies, 75
creoles, 75–77
crime, 5, 7–12, 17–19, 50,
52–53, 179–80
drug-related violence and,
52, 199
organized, 58, 173–77,
186–87, 197–99
undocumented immigrants
and, 53
See also drug cartels; drugs;
money laundering; violence
Cristero Rebellion, 74, 107, 109.
See also Catholic Church
CTM. *See* Mexican Federation
of Labor
cuisine, 193–95. *See also* culture
culture
drugs and, 186–87
indigenous Mexicans and, 64,
76–77, 103
Mexican Revolution and, 102–4
Mexico's colonial heritage
and, 69–74
and Mexico's impact on US
trends, 50–52, 193–95
and US impact on Mexico
trends, 50

See also architecture; art, arts;
  cuisine; muralists; music
currency, 28. *See also* economics;
  economy

de la Madrid, Miguel, 127–28, 130,
    137–38, 203
  drugs and, 6, 176
  Mexico's democracy and,
    47, 128–29
  poverty levels and, 22, 128–29
  reforms of, 127
democracy, 12, 42, 53
  1988 presidential race
    and, 132–33
  1994 presidential race and, 38,
    143–44, 153
  2000 presidential race and, 20,
    147–48, 153–54, 178
  2006 presidential race and, 178
  defining of, 39, 177–78
  drugs and, 173–77, 199–201
  future and, 171, 178–80, 201
  measuring degree of, 177–80
  Mexican Revolution and,
    97–98, 100–2
  Mexico's commitment to, 38–43,
    177–80, 201
  Mexico's consolidation of, 39,
    199–201
  Mexico's expectations
    of, 178–80
  Mexico's transition to, 39–43,
    47, 130–49
  NAFTA negotiations and, 26,
    130–33, 135–37
  private sector and, 134, 158–59
  See also Democratic Current;
    pluralism; politics
Democratic Current, 134. *See also*
  democracy
demographic distribution, 28–29

developing countries, 33. *See also*
  Latin America
Díaz Ordaz, Gustavo, 116, 118,
  121, 203
Díaz, Porfirio, 85–86
  Constitutions and, 84–85
  and the economic development
    of Mexico, 49, 86–88
  and the evolution of modern
    political structures, 71,
    85–88, 104
  Mexican Revolution and, 71,
    78–79, 91
  Mexico's colonial heritage
    and, 70–71, 75
  United States and, 49, 98
  See also politics; Porfiriato
Dirty War, 41, 122–23. *See also*
  human rights; military
discrimination, 51*t*, 190–93.
  See also tolerance
domestic violence, 189. *See also*
  violence; women
drones, 15. *See also* drugs;
  military
drug addiction, 185. *See
  also* drugs
drug cartels, 4–14, 17–19, 169,
  173–76, 186–87. *See also*
  corruption; crime; drugs;
  money laundering; political
  sovereignty
Drug Enforcement Agency, 8, 13,
  176. *See also* drugs
drugs
  domestic consumption of, 6,
    175, 185
  future and, 198–201
  legalization of, 175
  Mexico's democracy
    and, 197–99
  in Mexico's history, 3, 20

Mexico's political sovereignty
and, 17–18
religion and, 175, 177, 186–87
statistics and public opinion
on, 173–76
US and, 3–6, 11, 176
violence and, 3–5, 7–10,
169, 174–75
war on, 5, 173–76
See also crime; drug cartels;
Drug Enforcement Agency
drug-trafficking organization
(DTO), 10, 13, 176. *See also*
drug cartels; drugs
DTO. *See* drug-trafficking
organization

Echeverría, Luis, 122–23,
126, 203
EcoBici, 35. *See also*
environmental issues
Economic Commission for Latin
America (CEMLA), 33
economic recession of 2008, 53, 57.
See also economics, economy;
recessions
economics, economy
bank nationalizations and,
31, 126–28
crises in the, 17, 23,
128–29, 148–49
current state of the, 28–30, 180
environmental issues
and, 27, 65
growth of the, 16, 27–28, 45–46,
57–58, 95, 118–19, 128–29, 180
immigration and the, 50, 52–55,
58, 86, 199
Liberal-Conservative conflicts
and, 73–74, 78–79
Mexican Revolution
and, 89–102
Mexico's colonial heritage
and, 69–77

Mexico's democracy
and, 178–80
Mexico's economic miracle,
32, 118–19
Mexico's model for,
30–34, 135–37
NAFTA and, 25–28, 135–37
neoliberal, 134, 138, 140
public opinion on, 166
reform of, 31, 127–28, 180–82
and the relationship between
Mexico and the United States,
24–25, 57–59
role of Catholic Church
in, 73–76, 81–83, 85, 144–45,
159, 185
social inequality and, 20–24, 28,
95, 118–19
structural change in, 95–97,
135–39, 158–61
training in, 33, 137–39
US-Mexican relations
and, 130–31
violence and, 19, 94–97, 173–77,
197–201
See also banks, banking;
currency; industrialization;
investment; North American
Free Trade Agreement;
technocrats
education
drug prevention and, 58
and the evolution of modern
political structures, 79, 88, 96,
101, 160
Mexican Revolution and,
96, 103
Mexico's democracy and, 29,
116, 181–82
Mexico's economic model and,
118, 130, 137–39
poverty and, 23, 118, 181
role of the Catholic Church in,
74, 79, 144

social inequality and, 53–54, 181
Tlatelolco student massacre
    and, 120–22
tolerance and, 190–91
US-Mexican relations and, 23,
    53–54, 58
of women, 190
effective suffrage principle, 45,
    79, 87, 91. *See also* elections,
    electoral reforms
ejido system, 96–97. *See also*
    agriculture; land, land
    ownership
Elba Gordillo, Esther, 160
El Chamizal dispute, 56
elections, electoral reforms, 38,
    87, 171–73
    of 1964, 120, 123–25
    of 1988, 43, 47, 117, 120, 130–33,
        135, 143, 155
    of 1994, 26, 38, 43, 143–44
    of 2000, 153–54, 163, 172, 180
    of 2006, 163–65, 167,
        172–73, 179
    of 2012, 167, 168–71, 173, 179–80
    Mexico's democracy and, 38–
        40, 143–44, 153–82
    See also democracy; politics
Electoral Tribunal of the Federal
    Judiciary, 40, 147, 164, 172
El Paso, Texas, 11, 56. *See also*
    Ciudad Juárez
employment
    and attitudes toward gender
        roles, 188–90
    drugs and, 58, 199
    future and, 196–202
    immigration and, 25, 52–55
    Mexico's democracy and,
        90, 102
    NAFTA and, 24–28, 135–37
    public opinion on, 16t
    unemployment and, 16t,
        17, 149

See also economics, economy;
    labor rights
entrepreneurial families, 32,
    75. *See also* capitalism;
    entrepreneurs
entrepreneurs, 60, 75, 95,
    136. *See also* capitalism;
    entrepreneurial families
environmental issues
    global, 65–66
    NAFTA and, 26–27
    pollution and, 34–37, 65–66
    See also cars; natural resources;
        pollution
Environmental Protection
    Agency (EPA), 36. *See also*
    environmental issues
Estonia, 61
Europe
    links with, 25–26
    Mexico's colonial heritage
        and, 69–77
    See also European Union
European Union, 25–26, 135–36.
    See also Europe
extortion, 13, 19, 169, 174. *See also*
    crime; drug cartels
EZLN. *See* Zapatista Army of
    National Liberation

families
    capitalist, 32, 75–76, 86,
        95, 159
    drugs and, 13, 187
    Mexico's colonial heritage
        and, 61–62, 75–77
    Mexico's democracy and,
        25, 62, 95
FARC. *See* Revolutionary Armed
    Forces of Colombia
Federal Conciliation and
    Arbitration Board, 111.
    See also labor unions
Federal District, 166, 168

Federal Electoral Court, 161
Federal Electoral Institute (IFE),
     143, 147–48, 172, 182
   members and functions
     of, 143–44
   Mexico's democratic
     consolidation and the, 134–35
   See also National Electoral
     Institute
Federal Institute for Access
     to Public Information
     (IFAI), 156
Federal Reserve Bank of
     Mexico, 55
Federal Security Agency, 123
Félix Gallardo, Miguel
     Ángel, 13. *See also* drug
     cartels; drugs
Fernández del Cevallos,
     Diego, 143
financial institutions. *See* banks,
     banking
Flores Magón brothers,
     Ricardo and Enrique, 99
food, 194. *See also* culture
foreign debt, 82, 128, 148–49.
     See also economics,
     economy
foreign investment, 49–50,
     57–58, 60, 86, 136, 182. *See
     also* economics, economy;
     investment; manufacturing;
     remittances
Foundation for Sustainable
     Development, 36
Fox, Vicente, 4, 9, 43, 148, 155–56,
     163, 165, 203
   background of, 153–56
   drug cartels and, 4, 173–75
   Mexico's democracy
     and, 38, 43
   poverty and, 20–21
   See also Friends of Fox; politics
France, 78, 82–85

French-Conservative alliance, 78,
     82. *See also* France
Friends of Fox, 155, 157–58. *See
     also* Fox, Vicente

gangs, 11, 17, 199. *See also* crime;
     drug cartels
Garrido, Luis Javier, 107
gendarme units, 177, 197.
     See also military; police
gender, gender roles
   Mexican attitudes toward,
     188–190
   tolerance and, 190–93
   See also homosexuals; same-sex
     marriage; women
geography, 49–52. *See also* Mexico,
     Mexicans
Germany, 60
global warming, 36
Gómez Morín, Manuel, 106, 119,
     162. *See also* politics
González, Abraham, 93
González, Manuel, 85
Green Ecological Party of Mexico
     (PVEM), 36, 157
Guadalupe Hidalgo,
     Treaty of, 80. *See also*
     Mexican-American War
Guanajuato, 153, 155
Guatemala, 201
Guerrero, 19, 41, 62–63,
     123, 175–76
guerrilla groups, 93, 97
   Dirty War and, 122–23
   Mexico's democratic transition
     and, 97–98, 123, 140–42
   Zapatista uprising and, 140–42
   See also military; Zapatista
     Army of National
     Liberation
Guillermoprieto, Alma, 187
Gulf Cartel, 13. *See also* drug
     cartels

guns, 11. *See also* crime; drug
    cartels; violence

health, health care
    access to, 61, 53, 61
    poverty and, 21–22
    remittances and, 54
    See also social issues, social
        programs
Helms, Jesse, 47
Henríquez Guzmán,
    Miguel, 133
Heroic Military College, 44, 97.
    See also military
Hewlett Foundation, 177
Hidalgo, 63
Homeland Security Department,
    US, 10, 54. *See also*
    United States
homosexuals, 191. *See also* gender,
    gender roles
housing
    inequalities in, 61–62
    remittances and, 54, 58
    See also social issues, social
        programs
Huerta, Victoriano, 92–93, 99–100
human rights, 174, 185
    abuses of, 4, 20, 41, 45, 123,
        140–42, 174–75, 185
    agreements, 131
    legal system and, 41–42
    Mexico's democracy
        and, 39–41, 181, 185
    public opinion on, 184*t*, 198
    See also military; security;
        violence
human trafficking, 174.
    See also drug cartels;
    human rights

IFAI. *See* Federal Institute for
Access to Public Information
IFE. *See* Federal Electoral Institute

immigrants, immigration
    future and, 199
    illegal, 25, 53, 57, 198–99
    laws that govern, 53–54
    to Mexico, 45
    reform on, 53–55, 58
    US and, 25, 50, 52–55, 198
    See also refugees;
        undocumented immigrants
import substitution
    industrialization (ISI), 33
income
    of indigenous Mexicans,
        59, 62–63
    Mexico's democratic
        consolidation and, 171
    NAFTA and, 25–28, 33
    poverty and, 20–23, 59, 199
    public opinion and, 65, 191
    remittances and, 54, 58
    social inequality and, 28, 34, 61
    US-Mexican relations and,
        24–25, 49
    working-class, 33
    See also economics, economy;
        poverty
India, 29
indigenous Mexicans, 63–64, 86
    culture and, 64, 102–4
    Mexico's colonial heritage
        and, 69–73, 75–77
    social inequality of, 62, 77,
        140, 192–93
    See also poverty; Zapatista
        Army of National Liberation
industrialization, 32–33, 35, 118,
    159. *See also* economics,
    economy; manufacturing;
    urbanization
INE. *See* National Electoral
    Institute
inequality, 28, 61–63, 77, 140,
    177–78. *See also* indigenous
    Mexicans; poverty;

social development;
social justice
inflation, 16t, 118, 128, 149, 179.
    See also economics, economy
infrastructure, 17, 118.
    See also industrialization;
    transportation; urbanization
Institutional Revolutionary Party
    (PRI), 12, 30–31, 38–43, 160,
    164, 180–81
    decline of the, 117, 120–29
    electoral fraud by the, 139, 143
    electoral reforms of the,
        38–39, 188
    and modern political
        structures, 46–47, 105–7,
        116–17, 138
    electoral win in 2012 of
        the, 168–71
    evolving name of the, 44–46,
        105–8, 119, 162
    future of the, 116–17
    Mexico's democracy and the,
        40, 81, 132–33, 143–44
    Mexico's semi-authoritarian
        model and
        the, 123, 130, 146
    women and the, 188
    See also Mexican Revolution;
    politics
intellectuals, 90, 121–22, 162–63.
    See also universities
Inter-American Commission on
    Human Rights, 174. See also
    human rights
Inter-American Development
    Bank, 23, 59. See also banks,
    banking; economics,
    economy; Latin America
interest groups, 159–61. See also
    politics
International Boundary and
    Water Commission, 55–57.
    See also water

International Monetary Fund, 149.
    See also economics, economy;
    Mexican bailout
Internet
    Mexico's democratic
        consolidation and the,
        165, 171
    Mexico's democratic transition
        and the, 140, 142
    transparency and the, 157
    Zapatistas and the, 140, 142
    See also media
investment
    Díaz and, 49, 86
    in education, 29, 34, 88, 118
    Mexico's democratic transition
        and, 135–37
    Mexico's economic model
        and, 31–32
    NAFTA and, 24–25, 27, 57, 136
    US-Mexican relations and,
        49–50, 58, 60
    See also economics, economy;
    foreign investment;
    manufacturing
ISI. See import substitution
    industrialization
Islam, 71
Iturbide, Agustín de, 70

Japan, 59–60
Joint Operating Environment,
    Challenges and Implications for
    the Future Joint Force, 17
journalists, 8–9, 162, 186. See
    also media
Juárez, Benito, 78, 81–82, 85, 91.
    See also politics
Juárez Cartel, 7, 13. See also drug
    cartels
judiciary. See legal system

kidnapping, 13, 18–19, 169, 174,
186. See also crime; drug cartels

Knights Templar, 13. *See also* drug cartels

Labastida, Francisco, 153–54
labor market regulations, 26, 28–29. *See also* economics, economy
labor rights, 26, 90, 110–11. *See also* employment; labor unions; Mexican Revolution; working class
labor unions, 108, 110–11, 129, 159–60, 180. *See also* labor rights; working class
land, land ownership, 56, 96–97
  Catholic Church and, 75, 83
  Díaz and, 86, 90
  distribution of, 110, 133
  Mexican Revolution and, 92–94, 96–97, 101
  Mexico's colonial heritage and, 75–77
  See also agriculture; *ejido* system; peasants
Lasacell, 29
La Santa Muerte, 187. *See also* culture; religion
Latin America, 24, 41–43, 61, 111, 113, 180, 183, 189, 196, 201–2
Latin American Public Opinion Project, 178, 201. *See also* Latin America
Latinobarómetro survey, 154
Lawrence, D. H., 103
Left, 46, 121–22, 133–35, 163. *See also* politics; Right
legal system
  future and the, 197
  Mexico's democracy and the, 39, 41–42
  reforms of the, 41, 147–48, 181
  See also Mexican Supreme Court

Lerdo de Tejada, Sebastián, 85
Ley Iglesias, 83
Ley Juárez, 83
Ley Lerdo, 83
Liberals, Liberal Party
  conflicts between Conservatives and, 73–74, 78–88
  and Constitution of 1857, 74, 79, 83–85
  Mexico's colonial heritage and, 73–74
  and War of the Reform, 81–83
  See also Conservatives; politics
liberty, 177–79. *See also* democracy
literature, 102–3. *See also* art, arts
López Mateos, Adolfo, 118
López Obrador, Andrés Manuel (AMLO), 161, 166–68, 172–73
  background of, 166
  Mexico's democratic consolidation and, 135, 163–64
  poverty and, 166, 179
López Portillo, José, 128, 203
  electoral reforms of, 124
  nationalism of, 111
  nationalizing banks of, 31, 112, 126–27, 136
Los Tigres del Norte, 194. *See also* music
Los Tucanes, 187. *See also* music; *narco corridos*
Los Zetas, 10, 13

MacArthur, General Douglas, 113
Madero, Francisco I., 42–43, 91–92
  Mexican Revolution and, 43, 91–92
  murder of, 92, 99
  See also Anti-Reelectionist Party; Mexican Revolution; politics
Madrazo, Roberto, 164, 166
manufacturing

Conservatives and, 82
economic growth
   and, 118, 159
NAFTA and, 27–28
pollution and, 35
See also economics, economy;
   industrialization; investment;
   urbanization
marriage, 101, 185, 188–89.
   See also gender, gender
   roles; same-sex
   marriage; women
Maximilian, Emperor of Mexico,
   82. *See also* France
media, 167
   drug cartels and the, 162,
      175, 187
   economic crisis and the, 128
   Mexico's democracy and the,
      40, 48, 161–62
   US-Mexican relations and the,
      47–48, 55
   Zapatistas and the, 140, 142
   See also Internet; journalists;
      social media
Mérida Initiative, 15
mestizos, 63, 75–77
Mexican Air Force, 15, 113. *See also*
   military
Mexican-American War, 47, 50,
   79–81. *See also* Guadalupe
   Hidalgo, Treaty of
Mexican Army, 3, 6, 12, 15, 80,
   123, 173–77. *See also* military
Mexican Association of
   Businessmen (Coparmex),
   19, 158–59. *See also* business,
   businesses; Mexican Council
   of Businessmen
Mexican bailout, 148–49. *See
   also* economics, economy;
   International Monetary Fund
Mexican Council of Businessmen,
   159. *See also* business,

businesses; Mexican
   Association of Businessmen
Mexican Federation of Labor
   (CTM), 108. *See also* labor
   rights; labor unions
Mexican Navy, 14–15, 175. *See also*
   military
Mexican Revolution, 45, 89–129
   beneficiaries of the, 94–97
   causes of the, 89–91, 110
   civil-military relations altered
      by the, 43–45
   Constitutions and the, 74, 100–2
   cultural impact of the,
      102–4, 186
   Díaz and the, 78–79, 90–92
   economic growth and the,
      75–76, 95–97
   evaluating the results of the,
      38–39, 43–45, 94–98
   ideology of the, 79, 91, 116
   immigration and the, 52
   Madero and the, 91–92
   Mexico's colonial heritage and
      the, 73–77
   motto in the, 79, 91
   political institutions altered by
      the, 78–81
   political stability and the, 45–
      46, 91–98, 105
   structural change and
      the, 95–97
   United States and the, 98–100
   See also Madero, Francisco
      I.; Villa, Pancho; violence;
      working class
Mexican Supreme Court, 111, 147,
   175, 188–89, 191–92. *See also*
   legal system
Mexico City, 167
   drug cartels in, 11, 13
   earthquake in, 129
   Mexico's democratic
      consolidation and, 159, 167

party bureaucracy in, 125
pollution in, 34–36
violence in, 121, 123, 186
  See also Mexico, Mexicans;
    urbanization
Mexico, Mexicans
  challenges for, 16*t*, 42, 178–80
  church and state in, 71–73, 131
  colonial heritage of, 69–77
  democratic transition
    of, 130–49, 153–82, 199–201
  demographic growth of,
    28–30, 36, 63
  economic development
    of, 20–37, 45–49, 57–60,
    75–76, 118–19
  economic model of,
    30–34, 135–37
  flag of, 117
  foreign income of, 54–55, 58
  geography of, 49–52
  government of, 14, 22, 38–48
  governorships won by
    opposition parties in, 139–40
  history of, xvii–xviii, 69–149
  independence achieved
    by, 70–71
  nationalism in, 50, 82,
    84, 110–11
  political map of, xiv*m*, xv*m*
  possible collapse of,
    17–19, 174–75
  relations with the United States
    of, 14–17, 49–60, 197–99
  rural, 21, 56, 86, 118, 136–37
  security and violence in, 3–19,
    45, 50, 122–23, 173–76, 197–99
  semi-authoritarian model of, 38,
    42, 125–26, 179
  view of Americans by, 51*t*
  See also geography; Mexican
    Air Force; Mexican Army;
    Mexican Navy
Michoacán, 13, 19

middle class, 90, 95, 115–16.
  See also Mexican Revolution;
    social classes
military
  Díaz and the, 84–86
  drugs and the, 4–6, 174
  and the evolution of modern
    political structures, 43–45,
    97, 108
  Fox and the, 4, 174
  future and the, 197–98
  human rights violations of the,
    41, 140–42, 175, 185
  Mexican Revolution and the,
    45, 93–94, 97–98
  Mexico's colonial heritage and
    the, 70, 77, 83
  Mexico's democracy and the,
    40, 42–45, 142
  professionalization of the, 44–45,
    114, 126, 177
  relations between civilian
    leaders and the, 43–45,
    113–14, 141–42
  Tlatelolco student massacre and
    the, 141
  US Northern Command and
    the, 14–15
  and the War of Reform, 82–83
  World War II and the, 112–13
  Zapatista uprising and the, 26,
    64, 121–22
  See also gendarme units; Heroic
    Military College; security;
    violence
mines, mining, 49, 89–90. *See also*
    economics, economy
minority groups, 190–93. *See also*
    same-sex marriage; tolerance
money laundering, 10–11. *See also*
    crime; drug cartels
monopolies, 29–30, 160, 181. *See
    also* business, businesses
Monterrey, 159

Morena, 135, 167, 171, 173. *See
also* López ObradorAndrés
Manuel; politics
morphine, 12. *See also* drug
cartels; drugs
Movement for Renovation.
See Morena
municipalities, 7, 18, 23, 62–64,
137, 141, 174. *See also* poverty;
urban areas
Muñoz Ledo, Porfirio, 132. *See
also* politics
muralists, 102–4, 193. *See also*
culture
music
drugs and, 186–87
impact of Mexican Revolution
on, 102–4
and Mexico's impact on US
cultural trends, 52, 194–95
See also culture

NAFTA. *See* North American Free
Trade Agreement
narco corridos, 186–87. *See also
corridos*; music
National Action Party (PAN), 11,
40, 106, 123, 127, 147, 155–59,
164–68, 172
and the evolution of modern
political structures,
46–47, 119–20
Mexico's democracy and the,
38, 40, 120, 131–33, 143,
153, 180
political stability and the, 46
See also politics
National Addiction Survey, 175
National Autonomous University
of Mexico (UNAM),
115, 120–21
National Council to Prevent
Discrimination, 192. *See also*
discrimination

National Defense Secretariat,
Mexican, 14, 112, 142. *See also*
military
National Electoral Institute (INE),
40, 143, 171–73. *See also*
Federal Electoral Institute
National Executive Committee
(CEN), 108
National Federation of Peasant
Societies, 123
National Federation of Popular
Organizations (CNOP), 108
nationalism, 50, 82, 84, 110–11. *See
also* Mexico, Mexicans
National Liberation
Movement, 133
National Museum of
Anthropology and History,
64. *See also* culture
National Party of the Revolution
(PNR), 98, 109, 119
and the evolution of modern
political structures, 46, 105,
107–8, 114–16
Mexico's democracy and the, 44
See also politics
National Peasant Federation
(CNC), 108. *See also* labor
rights; labor unions
National Preparatory School, 115
National School of
Economics, 138
National School of
Engineering, 89
National School of Law, 115, 137
National System of Public
Security, 5
National Teachers Union
(SNTE), 160
natural resources, 30, 36,
55–56, 101. *See also*
environmental issues
Nava Martínez, Salvador, 139
Nebraska, 60

Nevada, 80
New Granada, 70
New Hampshire, 59
New Mexico, 59, 73, 80, 94
New Spain
    control of, 73
    economic system of, 75–76
    Mexico's colonial heritage
        and, 69–77, 103
    See also Mexico, Mexicans
New Yorker, 194
New York Times, 48
Nexos, 163
NEXTEL, 29
Niños Heroes, Los, 80
Nixon, Richard, 6
nongovernmental organizations
    (NGOs), 48, 66, 141, 156–57
nonintervention, 84, 112
NORAD. *See* North American
    Aerospace Defense
    Command
no-reelection principle, 87,
    125, 181. *See also* elections,
    electoral reforms; politics
North American Aerospace
    Defense Command
    (NORAD), 15
North American Development
    Bank, 37
North American Free Trade
    Agreement (NAFTA)
    economics and the, 25–28,
        33, 135–37
    Mexico's democracy and the,
        129, 131
    opposition to the, 140–41
    poverty and the, 22
    public opinion on the, 136
    US-Mexican relations and, 25–28,
        48, 57–59, 129
    See also economics, economy;
        Mexico, Mexicans;
        United States

Northern Command, US, 14–15.
    See also military; security

Oaxaca, 62–64, 81, 85, 141
Obama, Barack, 3, 58. *See also*
    United States
Obregón, Álvaro
    assassination of, 98, 104–5, 107
    Constitution of 1917 and, 87
    and the evolution of modern
        political structures, 104–7,
        110, 113–15
    Mexican Revolution and,
        79, 93–95
    See also politics
oil. *See* petroleum, petroleum
    industry
opium poppies, 12, 113. *See*
    also drugs
Oportunidades, 22, 57, 179,
    196–97. *See also* poverty
Orozco, Pascual, 92–93
Outline of Mexican Popular Arts
    and Crafts (Porter), 104
OXXO, 60

Pact for Mexico, 29, 32, 87, 160,
    180–82, 197, 202. *See also* politics
PAN. *See* National Action Party
Pani, Alberto J., 106
Parametría polling firm, 31, 191
Party of the Democratic
    Revolution (PRD), 121,
        133–35, 163, 165, 168
    Mexico's democracy and the,
        40, 131, 133–34, 143, 172
    political stability and the, 46
    See also politics
Party of the Mexican Revolution
    (PRM), 108, 116, 119, 157. *See*
    also politics
peasants, 97, 133, 140–41. *See*
    also agriculture; land, land
    ownership; poverty

PEMEX. *See* Petróleos Mexicanos
Peña Nieto, Enrique, 4–6, 9, 14,
      32, 41, 138, 160, 167–71, 177,
      180–81, 191, 198, 203. *See also*
      politics
peninsulares, 75–77
Pershing, John 'Black Jack', 94
Peru, 70
Petróleos Mexicanos (PEMEX), 31,
      60, 111
petroleum, petroleum industry, 58
   and the evolution of modern
      political structures, 110–12
   Mexico's economic crisis
      and, 127
   Mexico's economic model
      and, 30–34
   nationalization of, 30, 110–12
   See also economics, economy;
      natural resources
Pew Research Center Foundation,
      27, 53, 191, 194
Philippines, 69
Plan de Tuxtepec, 85
Plumed Serpent, The
      (Lawrence), 103
pluralism, 47, 134. *See also*
      democracy
plurinominal system, 124, 188.
      See also Chamber of Deputies
PNR. *See* National Party of the
      Revolution
police
   corruption of the, 18, 177
   drugs and the, 173–74, 186
   local, 8–9, 201
   Mexico's democratic
      consolidation and the, 200–1
   Mexico's possible collapse and
      the, 176–77
   and relations between military
      and civilian leaders, 176–77
   See also drugs; gendarme units;
      military; security; violence

political institutions, 97–98. *See
      also* military; politics
political sovereignty
   drugs and, 12, 17–19
   US-Mexican relations and,
      17, 198–99
   See also crime; drug cartels;
      politics; security
politics
   Catholic Church and, 43,
      71–74, 144–45
   civilian leadership in, 113–14
   Constitutions and, 30, 74,
      79, 83–89, 92, 100–6,
      110, 145
   Díaz and, 71, 85–88, 104
   electoral democracy and, 143–44,
      153–54, 177–80
   environmental issues and,
      34–37, 65–66
   Juárez and, 78, 81–82, 85, 91
   Liberal-Conservative conflicts
      and, 73–74, 78–88
   Mexican Revolution and, 45–46,
      78–81, 91–98, 105
   Mexico's colonial heritage
      and, 69–77
   Mexico's democratic
      consolidation and, 38–42
   Mexico's democratic transition
      and, 42–43
   military leaders and, 43–45,
      97–98, 108
   NAFTA and, 25–28, 135–37
   Pact for Mexico and, 180–82
   post-1920 evolution of, 104–20
   stability and, 45–46
   US-Mexican relations and, 46–48
   See also Chamber of Deputies;
      Congress, Mexican;
      Constitutions, Mexican;
      democracy; military;
      political institutions; political
      sovereignty; Senate

Polk, James K., 79–80. *See also*
    Mexican-American War
pollution, 34–37, 65–66. *See also*
    environmental issues
Pope Francis, 185. *See also*
    Catholic Church; religion
Porfiriato, 79, 85–88, 90, 110.
    See also Díaz, Porfirio
Porter, Katherine Anne, 103
Portes Gil, Emilio, 43, 107, 113–14.
    See also politics
Potosino Civic Front, 139
poverty, 16*t*, 16–24, 28, 34, 57–65, 97
    absolute, 20–21, 119
    addressing the issue of, 21–24,
        57, 166
    alleviation of, 179, 181
    Catholic Church and, 185
    defining of, 20–21, 119
    future and, 196, 198–99
    Mexico's democracy and,
        149, 178–80
    NAFTA and, 22, 25–28, 185
    social inequality and, 28, 63–64
    statistics and public opinion on,
        199–201
    US and, 58
    See also asset poverty; crime;
        social issues, social programs
PRD. *See* Party of the Democratic
    Revolution
*Presidential Succession of 1910,
    The* (Madero), 91. *See also*
    Madero, Francisco I.
PRI. *See* Institutional
    Revolutionary Party
PRM. *See* Party of the Mexican
    Revolution
Procampo, 59, 136. *See also*
    agriculture
Progresa, 22. *See also* poverty
Prohibition, 5. *See also*
    crime; drugs
Pronasol, 137

Pronatura, 66
Prospera, 22–23, 34, 57, 59, 196.
    See also poverty
Protestants, 185, 192–93. *See also*
    religion
Public Function, 201. *See also*
    corruption
PVEM. *See* Green Ecological
    Party of Mexico

Quintana Roo, 63

race, racism, 77, 191–92. *See also*
    Africa, Africans; indigenous
    Mexicans
railroads
    Díaz and, 49, 86, 110
    Mexican Revolution and, 89
    See also economics, economy;
        foreign investment
Rangel Mendoza, Bishop
    Salvador, 176
real estate. *See* land, land
    ownership
recessions, 21, 24–25, 53, 57,
    197, 199. *See also* economic
    recession of 2008; economics,
    economy
Reforma newspaper, 9.
    See also media
Reform Laws, 74
refugees, 50. *See also* immigrants,
    immigration
Regeneracíon, 99. *See also* media
regulations, 29, 66
religion, 183–87
    drugs and, 186–87
    freedom of, 71–73, 185
    Mexico's colonial heritage
        and, 71–74
    persecution based on, 192–93
    politics and, 144–45, 185–86
    public opinion on, 184*t*
    tolerance and, 185

See also Catholic Church
remittances, 25, 54–55, 58–59.
    See also foreign investment
Revolutionary Armed Forces of
    Colombia (FARC), 11. See also
    terrorists, terrorism
Revolution of 1910. See Mexican
    Revolution
Right, 46. See also Left; military;
    politics
Río Blanco Mill strike, 90. See also
    labor rights; working class
Río de la Plata, 70. See also
    New Spain
Rio Grande, 55–56. See also
    International Boundary and
    Water Commission
Rivera, Diego, 102, 193. See also
    art, arts
Rodríguez, Abelardo, 113. See also
    politics
Roosevelt, Franklin D., 193.
    See also United States
Ruffo Appel, Ernesto, 139–40.
    See also politics
Ruiz Cortines, Adolfo, 118.
    See also politics
Russia, 61

Salinas de Gortari, Carlos, 6,
24–26, 127, 146, 148, 203
    and the evolution of modern
        political structures, 47, 137–39
    Mexico's democracy and, 43–48,
        115–17, 132
    Mexico's political model altered
        by, 43, 130–31
    NAFTA and, 25, 130–31
    US media and, 48
    See also North American Free
        Trade Agreement; politics
same-sex marriage, 191–92.
    See also gender, gender roles;
    marriage

San Angel Group, 163
San Luis Potosí, 91
San Luis Potosí, Plan of, 92. See
    also Madero, Francisco I.
Scott, Winfield, 80
Secretariat of Government, 172
Secretariat of National
    Defense, 14
security, 17–19
    drugs and, 18, 174–76
    Mexico's democratic
        consolidation and, 173–77
    Mexico's democratic transition
        and, 140–42
    poverty and, 179–80
    public opinion on, 179–80
    US-Mexican relations and,
        57–58, 197–99
    See also military; police;
        political sovereignty
Senate, 182. See also Chamber
    of Deputies; Congress,
    Mexican; politics
September 11 terrorist attacks,
    54. See also terrorists,
    terrorism
Serra Puche, Jaime, 28, 129, 137.
    See also North American Free
    Trade Agreement
Silva Herzog, Jesús, 138. See also
    technocrats
Sinaloa, 6, 153
Sinaloa Cartel, 7, 13. See also drug
    cartels
Siqueiros, David Alfaro, 102–3.
    See also art, arts
SNTE. See National
    Teachers Union
soccer, 10
social classes, 65, 96, 103, 121
    and the evolution of modern
        political structures, 96
    Mexican Revolution
        and, 103

Mexico's colonial heritage
and, 76–77
See also middle class;
working class
social development, 61–66, 87–88,
202. *See also* social issues,
social programs
social issues, social programs
Díaz and, 49, 86–88
economy and, 180–82
environmental issues and,
34–37, 65–66
future and, 180–82, 196–99
indigenous Mexicans and, 62,
77, 140, 192–93
inequality and, 28, 30, 61–63, 77,
140, 177–78
influence of Catholic Church
in, 185
Liberal-Conservative conflicts
and, 73–74, 78–88
Mexican Revolution and, 38–39,
43–45, 94–98
Mexico's colonial heritage
and, 69–77
Mexico's democratic
consolidation and, 39,
154, 166–67
Mexico's democratic transition
and, 133–38, 140–41
Mexico's economic crisis and,
16–17, 148–49
poverty and, 16*t*, 16–24, 28, 34,
57–65, 97
and the War of the
Reform, 81–83
See also social development;
social justice; women
social justice, 39–40, 89–91, 96–97.
See also inequality;
Mexican Revolution;
social issues, social
programs
social media, 171. *See also* media

social mobility, 21, 96. *See also*
social issues, social programs
social security, 30. *See also* social
issues, social programs
South America, 112, 122. *See also*
Latin America
South Dakota, 59–60
sovereignty. *See* political
sovereignty
Soviet Union, 42, 94
Spain, 28, 75–76, 78
Mexico's colonial heritage
and, 69–77
and the role of the Catholic
Church, 71–74
Spanish language, 52, 62–63
State Department, US, 111.
See also United States
St. Jude Thaddeus, 187. *See also*
culture; religion
sub-Saharan Africa, 62
Sustainable Human Development
Foundation, 66
Syria, 9
Székely, Miguel, 21

Tabasco, 166, 183
Tamaulipas, 19
Tamayo, Rufino, 193
tariffs, 33, 118. *See also* economics,
economy; trade
taxes
collection of, 23
Mexico's economic model and, 34
public opinion on, 184*t*
reform of, 30, 34
technocrats, 33, 116,
130–31, 137–39
definition of, 137
Mexico's democratic transition
and, 130
See also economics, economy
telecommunications, 182. *See also*
infrastructure

Televisa, 29
Telmex, 29
terrorists, terrorism, 10–11, 14, 54,
    184*t. See also* September 11
    terrorist attacks
Texas
    drugs and, 7–8, 11, 13
    immigrants in, 53
    Mexican-American War and,
        80–81, 99
    US-Mexican relations and,
        27, 56, 59
Tijuana, 101, 187
Tijuana Cartel, 13. *See also* drug
    cartels
Tlatelolco student massacre,
    120–22, 141. *See also* violence
tolerance, 154, 190–93. *See also*
    democracy; discrimination;
    minority groups
torture, 175. *See also* violence
tourism, 60
TPPA. *See* Trans-Pacific
    Partnership Agreement
trade
    ISI and, 33
    Mexico's democracy and, 26,
        130–33, 135–37
    Mexico's economic model and,
        30–34, 135–37
    US-Mexican relations and,
        47, 59–60
    See also economics, economy;
        North American Free Trade
        Agreement
Trans-Pacific Partnership
    Agreement (TPPA), 25, 27
Transparency International, 28
Transparency Law, 156–57
transportation, 21, 59, 118. *See also*
    infrastructure
Treaty of Guadalupe
        Hidalgo, 80. *See also*
        Mexican-American War

Trump, Donald, xvii, 27, 55
Tuxtepec, Plan de, 85
TV Azteca, 29

UNAM. *See* National
    Autonomous University
of Mexico
Underdogs, The (Azuela), 103
undocumented immigrants, 25,
    53–55, 57–58, 198–99.
    See also immigrants,
    immigration
UN Human Development Report,
    23. *See also* United Nations
UNITAS Gold exercises, 14. *See
    also* Mexican Navy
United Nations, 29, 33–34
United Nations Human
    Development Report, 62.
    See also United Nations
United Self Defense of Colombia
    (AUC), 11. *See also*
    terrorists, terrorism
United States
    border of Mexico and
        the, xviii, 3, 5, 7, 10,
        36, 55–57
    drugs and the, 3–6, 8,
        10–13, 197–99
    economy of the, 23–25, 57–60
    environmental issues and
        the, 35–37
    and the evolution of modern
        political structures of
        Mexico, 46–48
    and future challenges for
        Mexico, 197–99
    government of the, 11, 47
    immigration and the, 25, 50,
        52–55, 198
    Mexican-American War and
        the, 47, 80
    Mexican Revolution and
        the, 98–100

Mexico's colonial heritage and the, 71
Mexico's impact on cultural trends in the, 50–52, 193–95
Mexico's political development and, 46–48
Northern Command of the, 14–15
poverty and the, 29–30
relations between Mexico and the, 33, 49–60, 98–100, 136
religion and the, 71–72
tolerance and the, 190–91
view of Mexicans in the, 51*t*
World War II and the, 56, 112–13
See also democracy; North American Free Trade Agreement; Wall Street
universities, 46, 115, 120–22, 155, 163, 190. *See also* education; intellectuals
UN Peacekeeping Operations, 15. *See also* United Nations
urban areas, 62, 118. *See also* Mexico City; municipalities; urbanization
urbanization, 36–37, 118. *See also* industrialization; manufacturing; Mexico City
Uruguay, 175
US-Mexico Border Program, 36
US Treasury, 149. *See also* economics, economy; United States
Utah, 80

Vasconcelos, José
and the evolution of modern political structures, 115, 119, 162
and the public funding of artists, 103
See also politics

Vázquez Mota, Josefina, 167–68. *See also* politics
Vega, General Clemente, 20. *See also* Fox, Vicente
Venezuela, 165
venture capital, 30, 60. *See also* capitalism; economics, economy
Veracruz, 47, 63, 80, 99–100
viceroyalties, viceroys, 69–71. *See also* Spain
Villa, Pancho, 47, 92–94, 99–100
assassination of, 94
Mexican Revolution and, 93–94
See also Mexican Revolution
violence
decade of, 97
drug-related, 4–10, 52, 57–58, 169, 174, 186–87
economic cost of, 19
future and, 180, 197–201
Mexican Revolution and, 45, 95–97
Mexico's democracy and, 39, 179–80
political change and, 95–97
political stability and, 46
statistics on, 7–10, 23, 52–53
US-Mexican relations and, 50
women and, 189, 192
See also drug cartels; Mexican Revolution; military; police; torture
Virgin of Guadalupe, 185. *See also* Catholic Church; religion
voluntary organizations, 65–66
Vuelta, 163

Wall Street, 148–49. *See also* United States
Walmart of Mexico, 102. *See also* business, businesses
War of the Reform, 81–83
Washington Post, 163

water, 56, 61. *See also* International
     Boundary and Water
     Commission
Western Union, 54
West Rail Bypass International
     Bridge, 27
Wilson, Henry Lane, 99
Wilson, Woodrow, 99–100
women
   and attitudes toward gender
        roles, 188–90, 192
   education of, 190
   and femicide, 189
   Mexico's economic crisis
        and, 129
   Spanish, 76
   See also gender, gender roles;
        social issues, social programs
Woodrow Wilson Center's Mexico
     Institute, 27
working class, 89–90, 95–96, 110.
     See also labor rights; labor
     unions; Mexican Revolution;
     social classes
World Bank, 20, 23, 29, 62, 102, 118
World Economic Forum Global
     Competitiveness Index, 28
World Justice Project, 41

World Values Survey, 65, 183, 191
World War I, 93
World War II, 11–12, 52, 56, 112–13

Yaquis, 86. *See also* indigenous
Mexicans
Yucatán, 63, 86

Zacatecas, Battle of, 93
Zapata, Emiliano, 90, 92–93
Zapatista Army of National
     Liberation (EZLN)
   civil-military relations and
        the, 141–42
   indigenous Mexicans and,
        64, 122
   uprising of the, 26,
        140–41, 143–46
   See also Chiapas; indigenous
        Mexicans
Zedillo, Ernesto, 138, 146, 203
   drugs and, 6, 175–76
   on electoral reform, 39
   Mexican bailout and, 148–49
   Mexico's democracy and, 38–39,
        43, 143–44, 147–48
   poverty and, 21–22
   See also politics